A
VOICE
WAS
SOUNDING

SELECTIONS FROM *THIS LAND*

VOL
5

**THIS LAND
PRESS**

Works appearing in this anthology were originally
published between January and December 2014 in *This Land*, Tulsa, OK.

Vincent LoVoi, Publisher; Michael Mason, Editor.

WWW.THISLANDPRESS.COM

Book designed by This Land Press.
Printed in the United States of America.

First Edition, April 2015

ISBN: XXXXXXXXXXXX

PRAISE FOR *THIS LAND*

"A rare example of literary journalism... *The New Yorker*
with balls."
—*Columbia Journalism Review*

"I first discovered This Land Press in 2012, and I am so glad that
I did. In just a short time, they have created something special
not just for readers in Tulsa, but for the rest of us around the
world. With outstanding storytelling, thoughtful reporting, and
truly diverse voices, they've become a model for the future of
journalism with a real sense of place."
— Mark Armstrong, *Longreads*

"*This Land* suggests the kind of pioneering spirit that Woody
Guthrie would likely approve."
—*Monocle* magazine

"Nobody tells our story like *This Land.* In this eclectic and
compulsively readable volume, essays of character and place,
portrait and memoir, tightly researched journalism, and
delectable fiction all combine to create a whole that is much
larger than its parts. *A Voice Was Sounding* is a tapestry, a feast,
a tamed cacophony that evokes not merely the heartland of
America but its very heart: bitter, self-obsessed, self-deprecating,
glorious. Here is a collection of writings from the center of
America that is as disparate and wild and strange as the land
from which it springs."
— Rilla Askew, *Fire in Beulah*

"I love this!"
—David Carr, *The New York Times*

A
VOICE
WAS
SOUNDING

SELECTIONS FROM *THIS LAND*

VOL
5

CONTENTS

A
VOICE
WAS
SOUNDING

SELECTIONS FROM *THIS LAND*

VOL
5

INTRODUCTION

I'VE SEEN THE INSIDES OF SNAKE PITS and senators' offices. I've hunted rattlers in the western Oklahoma desert, used my hands to snatch catfish from lake bottoms, and hosted living-room conversations with movie stars. I've clung to cowboys on the backs of ATVs, helped Ethiopian women prepare a feast for 500, and held a 10-week-old tiger cub.

From my point of view, the best stories I've worked on aren't the ones that were written in an armchair—they're the ones that sent me into the field, out of my comfort zone, to talk to people I've never met. That's why I got into the news business.

My husband knows reporting was my first love—in fact, the first time I laid eyes on him was when I saw his picture on the front page of our local newspaper. But even as I courted this love, reporting the news for first an alt-weekly and then a business-to-business paper, I knew something was missing. In keeping up with the fast pace of the news cycle, in chasing other reporters to the scene, in making all those deadlines, I was missing out on the bigger story. I didn't want five minutes with a source, I wanted five hours, five days, because I knew the good stuff never came out in that first interview. I wanted more than a few column inches; I wanted the time and space to tell a story, to get into the details, to set the scene and develop the characters.

This Land magazine wasn't quite a year old when I found an opportunity to do both of the things I craved: report news, and also tell stories. I signed on as news editor of *This Land* in 2011, and for the last year, I've served as the magazine's managing editor. In this role, I try to pass on my passion for reporting to as many writers as possible.

In February of 2014, I received an email from a writer new to *This Land*, Jezy J. Gray. His first submission to us had been published in our Ralph Ellison issue—it was a retrospective look at Ellison's impact on the literary world, and the disregard Jezy felt Ellison was given by his high school history teacher, who doubled as a football coach.

Jezy was a good writer and an academic. He was finishing his master's degree in English and was about to begin a PhD program in Indiana. But before he went, he had an idea for another article: He wanted to write about the country's largest outdoor furry festival, which just happens to take place at a state park in southeastern Oklahoma every year. I'd been trying to get someone to write that story for a while.

Jezy had built a rapport with the festival's organizer—the group was understandably averse to media coverage, and we'd thus far failed to make any headway—and he'd agreed to give Jezy full access to the event.

But, Jezy told me, "I'm not a reporter." So we talked about reporting, about the details that bring a story to life. About how to take note of your surroundings so you can set the scene for your readers. About how what a person looks and sounds like when she's talking, the way her hands move and her face contorts, are just as important as what she's saying. We also talked about the craft of interviewing: when to ask questions, and when to be quiet and listen, and how to leave just enough silence that the subject feels compelled to fill it—with details he might not otherwise offer.

Through the editing process, I helped Jezy take all the things he saw and heard and smelled and shape them into a story, the kind that makes readers happy to be along for the ride.

The process took months, and the result, "Wild Life," which was published in September of 2014, is a nuanced account of the people who participate in the anthropomorphic arts, who toe that line between human and animal—some for fun, some for pleasure, and some because they truly believe there's a part of them that isn't human—and *This Land* was the first mainstream outlet (read: not connected to the furry community) to offer such an account.

It's a painstakingly reported piece that you'll find within these pages, among some of our other favorite stories published in 2014—stories of soccer stars and fan boys, tiger kings and televangelist heirs, Broadway writers and wannabe Indians. The contents of this anthology chronicle journeys far from home and illuminate the places closest to our hearts. It also contains profiles of four Oklahomans who, coincidentally, all celebrated centennials in 2014.

In the same year, we gave our web store a physical home in our Tulsa headquarters, released our first full-length documentary to the masses, and took a trip to New York City to share stories about Oklahoma with people who used to think of it as fly-over country but by the end of the night were asking when they could come visit.

For me, the most rewarding part of 2014 was helping writers and reporters develop those stories that made New Yorkers fall in love with Oklahoma and Oklahomans learn something about their state they hadn't known before, and to embrace it in all its beauty, strangeness, and contradictions. My hope is that these stories will inspire you to do the same, and to leave your armchair once in a while, reporter or not.

Holly Wall
Managing Editor

ONE

STATE OF PLAY

TO BOLDLY GO

An Oklahoma studio brings Star Trek fantasies to life.

By *Samuel Annis*

IT'S A STEEL-COLORED DECEMBER DAY, and I'm driving down OKC's May Avenue, past dirty snow and abandoned cantinas, looking for a roofing company. Actually, I'm looking for a non-profit Star Trek fan-film studio, but the man I contacted, Richard Wells, tells me that the studio's address is "jacked up," and suggests I drive to the roofers and call him from there.

Outside, the temperature is 30 degrees. A snowstorm swept through only a few days ago, and the city seems stunned. To say that Oklahoma doesn't thrive in winter is a vast understatement, and I pass only a few other cars wading through the gasoline-colored slush covering the road.

The fact that studio opened at all today surprises me.

It would be a lie to say I'm not already stereotyping the people I expect to meet there. The way Starbase Studios operates allows anyone with a script and a camera to come shoot his show/film/documentary/ Star Trek-themed wedding photos on the set for free, and therefore I suspect that the crowd will be composed of hardcore Roddenberry fans playing out their more beloved Trek fantasies.

I see the roofing company, and so I call Richard. He tells me to turn left down a certain street, and then to turn into the first lot on the right.

"I'll come out and meet you," he says.

What I take to be the first lot on the right is a parking area for an unremarkable and boring building that could hold anything from doctors to 3-D printers. I take a couple laps around the parking lot before it becomes clear that Richard is not here, but I do see a man in a down jacket standing on the other side of a hedge. I leave the asphalt and pull into an unplowed driveway. It leads to an abandoned-looking building and an open bay door, the narrowest I've ever seen. The man in the down jacket stands there, flagging me in.

Against the bitter whiteness of the snow, the space behind the open door looks like a hole in the world, black and empty.

The car fits with only inches to spare, and the door closes behind me. This space is dark, and I can barely make out the dim shapes of several cars, some steel poles holding a roof high above my head, and the reflection of low-watt bulbs in a puddle. I open the door and am met with a damp, earthy smell.

The man with the down jacket is standing near my door, hands in his pockets, tiredness obscuring the smile he gives me.

"Richard?" I ask.

"That's me," he says. "Welcome to Starbase."

———————

Once upon a time, a group of devoted Star Trek fans in Austin, Texas, decided they wanted to add to the Star Trek world by filming their own show. They built a few sets—a hallway, a bridge—and begin to film their show: Starship Exeter. Near the end of 2000, Exeter released one episode, and began work on a second, but it was never completed. In 2010, Oklahoma-native John Hughes (not to be confused with the writer/director of The Breakfast Club) purchased the badly damaged and fragmented version of the Exeter set and took it to an airplane hangar at El Reno Regional airport. Realizing he basically now owned a massive and incomplete Lego kit, Hughes posted an ad on Craigslist looking for people willing to volunteer their time to help him rebuild it. Among the volunteers were the two current managers of the studio: Scott Johnson and Richard Wells. Between Wells, Johnson, Hughes, and many other volunteers (the majority of whom still remain involved with the studio's productions), the pile of com-panels and Red Alert signs began resembling an actual bridge.

The volunteers decided the bridge should move to a more central location, so it was bisected, loaded back into a truck, and taken to its current OKC location.

As the work neared completion, Hughes handed the reigns over to Richard and Scott and began working on Starship Ajax,[1] his own show.

Under the eyes of the two new managers, Starbase Studios blinked into existence, and only two months into her working life, three projects have been filmed. The first was a fan show (created by Starbase volunteers from OKC) called Starship Valiant, the second was a documentary (sort of) from Lexington, Kentucky, called Hanlet: Episode 4 & ½: Attack of the Phantom Special, and the third is Yorktown: A Time to Heal, the production I'm here to observe.

We're making our way down a two-block-long corridor, wide as a three-lane highway. The smell of soil makes me feel like we're underground. Richard tells me shooting was supposed to begin the day before, but the snowstorm stranded half of the group in airports as they made their way down from Canada. Richard tells me they're in the process of shooting stills, trying to get back on schedule.

"How long are they going to work today?" I ask.

"11:00, maybe midnight. Maybe later."

"When did you get here?"

"I've been here since yesterday," he says. "I slept here."

The ceiling looms over our head, and thick, tubular lights drizzle a pale green sheen over antique and collectible cars parked on either side.

---

1 As of this writing, *Ajax* has yet to film, according to their Facebook page, due to "set issues."

He walks this path constantly and so none of this is unusual to him. For me, the incongruous collection of '20s gangster-mobiles and '60s hot-rods strike a peculiar tone. The past is retained here, stored for some unknown future date, but it is a past of no particular era, like generations of toys forgotten in a chest. When I ask, Richard tells me they rent the place from a guy who manages estate sales.

We walk forward one block and a few decades and the room brightens around clusters of '90s and '00s vans and SUVs.

Half a block later, the ceiling rises by 15 or so feet, and we are in a room similar to Kane's Xanadu storehouse: wall-to-wall antique bureaus, concrete statues, bird cages, desks, dressers, tables, a gigantic pair of plaster wings, bedframes, pinball machines, end tables, nightstands, and cardboard boxes full of items ever decreasing in size.

Three-quarters of the way through the room, a long plywood wall rises towards the warehouse ceiling. Beyond the wall, a series of blue tarps stretch like a Bedouin's tent, glowing with a cold brilliance from a hidden source of illumination.

More tarps form a curtain in the wall. Richard lifts a corner and I walk into a small room made entirely out of tarps.[2] A propane-fueled patio heater takes up a good quarter of the room, and some vacant folding chairs cluster around it.

This is one of only two heated spaces in the studio.

We pass through the tarp room and emerge into the space sectioned off by the plywood walls. Before me is what looks like a spaceship made entirely out of untreated lumber, computers, colored plastic squares, and electrical wires.

And that is exactly what it is.

A section of the bridge wall swings open, and a man wearing a yellow unitard trots out before he vanishes behind a door across the room from us.

Richard tells me that the Yorktown group is in the middle of taking stills, so he can't take me on the bridge quite yet. Instead, he shows me the outside. The most notable components of the construction are the

---

2 The studio uses tarps in a manner that can only be termed "comprehensive."

computers—mostly Dells, with monitors and keyboards attached to them—littering the wooden sides like cyber barnacles.

"There are maybe 57 of them," says Richard. "One went down last night due to the storm, and I was up until four in the morning replacing it with a spare." That explains why he looks tired.

A scruffy-looking man in glasses and a hoodie comes toward us. He's moving quickly and he starts talking in fast sentences. Does Richard know where the electrical tape is? Richard scans the piles of tools, extra lights, cables, and bags of Doritos cluttering every flat surface and says that he does not.

"Scott Johnson," Richard says by way of introduction. Scott tells me to wipe my feet on several different mats before walking onto the bridge, hands me a business card[3] with his name on it, and takes off.

Richard and Scott met years before John Hughes posted his ad on Craigslist, while both employed in the concert production industry. After they both became unable to work (Richard due to a mild case of narcolepsy, and Scott after a lighting truss collapsed on his shoulder), Richard saw Hughes' ad for volunteers and called Scott.

Both joined immediately, but for different reasons. Scott calls it "literally a dream come true." His enthusiasm for Star Trek shows in his semi-constant presence on the bridge. Richard, who admits to never having been a dedicated fan of the original show, badly wanted to do something other than sit around the house. Now that the bridge is mostly built, his participation plays out in the surprisingly gentle way that he takes care of the actors and crew.[4]

Although neither of them ever defined it as such, they clearly developed a degree of friendship over time that enables them to work well together and with a mutual trust that manifests itself in the way they stay out of one another's hair.

---

3 I received several business cards during that visit, which made me feel both oddly important and embarrassed that I didn't have cards of my own.

4 Later in my visit one of the actresses needs a computer to email potential employers and Richard gives her his laptop, endures the barrage of complaints she tosses at him regarding its age and inadequacy, and helps her send the emails.

We've made it halfway around the bridge when someone from inside shouts that they need the Red Alert lights turned on. Scott appears and asks me to pass him a hammer lying behind me on a shelf.

"For the lights?" I ask.

"No," he says. "I've been looking for it."

Then he shows me the Red Alert switch, which is, in fact, a light switch. He tells me that when they're filming, the way they get the Red Alert to flash is by having someone stand here and toggle the switch back and forth.

"As long as you can keep time and count to two," he says, "you can have this job."

The three of us stand in silence for a moment. We can hear someone on the bridge arranging people into futuristic tableaus. Richard tells me we're right outside the turbo lift.

"We can probably climb in there without disturbing the actors," he says, then opens a small door, and I follow him into the lift.

The floor is covered with miniature-golf-course grass, and the walls are painted gunmetal gray. With both of us in there, the room feels very small.

Rich starts to say something, but then the sliding doors in front of us open and we're on the bridge. A group of men in Starfleet uniforms is staring at us.

———————

"Can we walk around?" I ask Richard. "Are they finished taking photographs?" I want badly to sit in the chairs, to push the buttons, and to look at the various blinking and pulsing screens pretending to communicate something. I know this feeling. I remember it from being a child and finding an old computer or telephone in a junkyard. These objects always became temporary props in my imaginary games, and I would pretend to relay secret codes and type complex algorithms with a ferocity that surely alarmed my parents even though they never said anything about it.

This bridge, though, surpasses anything I ever dreamed up.

For one thing, there are no imaginary spaces. Imaginary spaces are spaces that can't be filled with the appropriate object to make the scene complete, so the object is mentally placed there. (When I used to play "Cowboys," for instance, imaginary spaces were the saloon, the dirt-covered street, the horse I rode, and basically everything except for maybe my cowboy hat.) Here, everything is where it should be: red and gold buttons, black chairs shaped like shoehorns, red banisters, switches, and, good lord, the scores of screens with swirling and blinking graphics going on them. It is a precise reconstruction of a starship bridge.

There's also this bizarre effect that they've achieved with their lighting that makes reality look different. I don't know if it results from the red, blue, and yellow color scheme, or if the construction lights reflect off the tarps in a profoundly Trekkian fashion, but I very much feel as though I'm in a different time, both in the past and the future.

John Carroll, the director of the scenes being shot, calls for a break before the actual filming begins, giving Richard and I free rein of the ship. Richard sits in one of the chairs and I stand, feeling overwhelmed. The only things shattering the illusion of the '60s vision of the 2300s are the huge stage lights and the ceiling made of tarps.

Richard is talking to me about the buttons on the ship.

"Each one," he says, "we made by hand." I look around me at the thousands of buttons and try to understand the tedium that job entailed.

He adds that they used ice-cube trays as molds to get the perfect square shape.

"What about the round buttons?" I ask.

"Those are marbles. Well, they're supposed to be marbles, but nobody makes the right size anymore so I wound up having to make them by hand too."

While we're here, John Carroll and the producer/force behind Yorktown, John Atkins, come back on board, and begin talking about camera angles and lighting. They're both young men, probably in their mid 30s. Carroll wears a large winter coat, but Atkins is dressed only in his red Starfleet uniform, which looks thin and unable to retain body heat. During a pause in their conversation I go over to talk with them.

"Why," I ask, "are you here? I get that it's to finish this film, but why are you making it in the first place? It can't make any money,[5] and it's not going to propel your careers forward."

Atkins and Carroll don't really need to think about the answer.

"For fun," Atkins says. "And a chance to finish something that began two decades ago."

"Were you fans of the original show?"

"I wasn't even alive when it was airing," Carroll says. "I've seen it, obviously, and I think it's great, but I'm not obsessed. This set though is amazing. By far one of the coolest experiences."

Carroll checks his watch and decides that the break is over. Because of the storm, the crew is far behind schedule and Carroll wants to see what they can do to get back on. Storming off the bridge, he opens the door to the green room where several actors are putting on costumes.

"Everyone on set," he says. "I want to start filming now."

Someone in the room complains of a wardrobe malfunction.

"Duct-tape it," shouts Carroll as the door slams behind him.

Richard and I leave the set, letting Atkins and Carroll finish setting up whatever it is they need to set up. Unlike most of the people at the studio, Richard doesn't seem interested in being a part of the films themselves. He doesn't even seem particularly intrigued by what happens on the bridge once the doors are closed, as though it's none of his business. When I first arrived, I asked if I could take his picture. He said yes, but seemed confused as to why I would want to, as though his role is so inconsequential that even a photograph stretches it out of proportion.

When most of the actors and studio personnel are warming up in the green room, I find Richard sitting in the tarp room by himself with his arms folded over his lap and thinking, perhaps, of the transporter room he'd like to build in the spring. Nevertheless, he always happens to

---

5 Due to the rigid nature of copyrights, any Star Trek-themed show, prop, costume, or idea not designed by the studio that owns the Star Trek license can't be used to make anybody any money.

be close by whenever anyone needed something, and I sense a distinctly dad-like aura around him, like he's allowing his children the freedom to play their games but always nearby if they need his help.

As the green room empties, Richard tells me I can warm up in there if I want. Yes, I realize, I'm extraordinarily cold. In my fascination with the bridge, I forgot that the warehouse and the bridge are, at best, a few degrees above freezing. Watching the men and women in their thin cotton unitards take their place on the starship bridge, I wonder how they're going to keep from shivering through the entire film.

In the green room, a man named Brian is looking through a pile of empty Pizza Hut boxes for a leftover slice. On the floor beside the boxes are two crates: one of them full of plastic phasers and scanners, the other full of fake noses and ears.

I spend a large chunk of the day in this room, warming up between short excursions into the area surrounding the bridge where several bags of chips have been left on a table for snacking.

Because not everyone at the studio needs to be on the set at all times, there are moments when the green room becomes full of people jockeying for position next to the electric heater. Some talk happens, but the walls to the room are thin sheets of plywood, and any noise louder than whisper will be picked up by the microphones outside. It's weird, but the situations where talking is prohibited are the moments where I think people find they have the most to say. Like any taboo, imposed silence exists only to be broken, and I feel like I'm participating in a slumber party, trying not to wake up any parents.

I'm thinking about looking to see if Brian missed a slice of pizza when the ground starts to shake. It feels like a train going by at a close distance. There are maybe five other people in the room including Richard and Scott, and their general calm (a look at the ceiling—unmoved facial expressions) leads me to believe that this is no more than a really, really stiff gust of wind.

"That was an earthquake," says Richard.

"Wait, really?" I am incredulous and extremely surprised.

"4.5," says Scott, looking into his phone. "Just north of Jones."

I don't know where Jones is, but obviously not far enough away. I look up and it strikes me for the first time how the ceiling 30 feet above us is really just a series of deadly glass panels. I wonder if we'll evacuate. Then I wonder if anyone cares. From the bridge, I can hear some jokes about being attacked by Klingons.

"I hope my house is still on the blocks," says Richard, and that is the last anyone says about it.

I step outside the green room and listen to the work being done on the bridge. I turn up the collar on my overcoat and think about those poor people in their cotton onesies who are doing this strictly for enjoyment.

Endemic Star Trek dialogue drifts through the walls:

"I'm detecting a small shuttlecraft approaching."

"Visual, please."

"It's federation approved."

They do take after five-second take of things like this, and I am riveted to the plodding repetition.

Richard comes out of the green room.

"You may be able to find a crack somewhere in the wall to see into the studio," he says, and then vanishes into the tarp room.

I walk around outside of the studio, looking for this elusive crack, trying to make as little noise as possible, and I almost fall into an enormous tub of candy left over from Halloween. Eventually, I find a vertical seam where a door hasn't been shut tightly enough, but all I can see is the top of one man's head and the ear of another.

They've moved on from the dialogue to a quick scene that shows the effects on the bridge when something blows up somewhere else on the ship: All the actors need to lurch simultaneously in the right direction, and afterwards, the captain needs to say, "What the hell was that?"

Carroll films the lurching maybe three times, and then they get to work on the "What the hell was that?" The actor playing the captain tries out many different sorts of inflections, ranging from "What the hell was that?" to "What the HELL was that!?" Throughout all of this, the bridge is full of people who never say a thing, the extras, so to speak, who are there purely to maintain visual accuracy, like the colorful buttons. Given the fact that these people traveled all the way from Austin or

Canada, their willingness to do virtually nothing for hours at a time is bewildering to me.

Later, when all the Yorktown crew except Atkins and Carroll are in the green room, I ask them about this. Their answers, all of them, sound remarkably familiar:

For fun.

I realize now that I don't understand what this means. For me, the idea of "fun" is elusive. Obviously I can tell you when I am having fun or when I'm not having fun, but the idea of "just for fun" doesn't much enter my mental space anymore. Everything I enjoy, everything, that is, I call "fun," also serves the double purpose of being edifying or self-improving in some way. The rule applies to my full range of activities: from reading to sex, "just for fun" is never just for fun.

One of the actors tries to get back on the bridge after using the bathroom,[6] and Scott rushes out from the tarp room, presumably to make sure they've wiped their feet, but also to help them with the door itself, which sticks. Its obvious how much he's in love with this place. This love may manifest itself differently from Richard's, might come across as more manic and hovering, but so does the love of most mothers I know.

There is one moment when both Scott and Richard are in the neutral space between the tent room and the green room. They stop and briefly discuss various upcoming things on the Starbase calendar. The moment is touching and oddly beautiful, like seeing the parents of a young family hug. The moment ends when Scott decides he really wants to see what's happening on the set, and scrambles up a nearby ladder while Richard and I watch from below.

"You won't see anything from up there," says Richard, meaning that the tarps hanging over the bridge will obscure the view, but Scott possesses in abundance the curiosity that Richard lacks. When I ask Richard about his vision for the studio, he tells me that he sees it moving into an outreach role, trying to reach more than just fan-filmmakers.

---

6 And by "bathroom" I mean the alley next to the warehouse or the Sonic across the street.

"I want interactive classes offered, and videos that can play on the bridge view-screen. Maybe a 'What is Sci-Fi' class or an educational YouTube series for kids."

The endgame for Richard is not to enter the world of Star Trek, but to enhance the world he lives in now.

A plane flies overhead and interrupts the shoot. Caught up in the world of the studio, I almost forgot that a reality exists outside of the warehouse. There are planes, and rocket ships, and people going to and returning from their jobs, their families, their lives. Some of them never take a break from that shuttling, and most of them probably look at places like Starbase as childish delusions, a waste of time.

It's easy to think our culture is not brimming with respect for a person who dresses up in costumes, puts on fake hair, and changes the shape of his/her nose to resemble somebody they are not, but that is not true. Ours is absolutely a culture that rewards these things. Why else would we idolize our movie stars? Why else would plastic surgery be an industry? Anyone attempting to deride or mock people wearing Vulcan ears or blue antennae should first consider their own hair-color treatments, Botox injections, liposuction sessions, protein shakes, tanning beds, tanning spray, facelifts, breast implants, bikini waxes, and juice diets. There is one crucial difference: the people at Starbase know they are playing.

I spend the next few hours in the green room, talking to the various crew members who've momentarily decided that, yes, it is cold as hell out there. The range of backgrounds and careers represented destroys the unfortunate impression I had of people who dress up like TV show characters. Among those present are electrical contractors, professional makeup artists, robot builders, software designers, and one woman who recently finished her master's degree in fashion. They are bright people, in many different senses of the word, and I feel a sense of warmth—not least because I am sitting closest to the space heater—from being with them. For a moment, I can almost imagine myself a part of their family.

Some bellowing outside the green room indicates that Carroll is ready to film again. The actors leave and I am left alone for a few moments. I figure that I've seen all that I can, and I go to find Richard. He is sitting alone in the tarp room, slouched contentedly in a folding chair. I tell him that I'm all set, and he stands, stretches, and leads the way out of the tarp room, back through the stacks of unsold furniture, and into the corridor with the cars. I can see my own car parked at the furthermost point of the warehouse.

I ask if he plans on going home early today, and he tells me, no, he'll stay until the shooting is finished. He says he should be here in case anything else goes wrong, but that sounds like an excuse. He's here because he can't imagine being anywhere else. It's clear in the gentle way he leans against the frame of the ship or in the careful way he stands back and looks at everyone rushing around in red unitards and rubber Vulcan ears: This is his home, and everyone else is a guest. He was here before they arrived, and he'll be here long after they're gone.

Richard and I shake hands, and as I climb into my car he opens up the bay door behind me. When I reverse into the winter evening, I see that it is snowing. I put the car in park and watch Richard close the door, his body vanishing piece by piece, until just his shoes are left, and then nothing.

BROADWAY'S
FORGOTTEN MAN

Everyone knows 'Oklahoma!,' but who's heard of Lynn Riggs?

By *Charles Morrow*

It's 1945, and our setting is a Christmas party in Manhattan. The celebrants are show-business professionals affiliated with the Theatre Guild, a company enjoying tremendous prosperity due to the phenomenal success of Rodgers and Hammerstein's stage musical *Oklahoma!,* which the Guild produced.

Audiences adored the show from the moment it opened on March 31, 1943, and it had played to packed houses ever since—not just in New York but across the U.S. and even overseas, where touring companies entertained U.S. troops. The production, which cost around $92,000 to mount (cheap for a musical even then), was grossing millions every year. Guild personnel had every reason to feel cheery, especially producer Theresa Helburn, who by all accounts was the single individual most responsible for the genesis and development of *Oklahoma!*

It was Helburn who believed in the project from the beginning and played a key role in hiring most of the show's gifted contributors—composer Richard Rodgers, lyricist/librettist Oscar Hammerstein, choreographer Agnes de Mille, and others—whose collaborative efforts resulted in an innovative musical milestone that broke many of the unwritten rules of genre, and established new ones. Thanks to *Oklahoma!,* the Guild, which had been on the brink of bankruptcy in the early '40s, was thriving. In the course of the holiday festivities, Helburn encountered a slender, bespectacled gent who was associated with the show, and jovially addressed him. "Where have you been keeping yourself, young man?" she asked. "You have been neglecting me terribly. Don't you realize, sir, that it was I who made it possible for you to become a Gentleman of Leisure?" The man smiled and replied, "I beg your pardon, but don't you realize it was I who made it possible for YOU to become such a Busy Madam?"

The speaker was neither Rodgers nor Hammerstein, and sure wasn't Agnes de Mille, and yet he spoke the truth. He was Lynn Riggs, poet and playwright, author of the stage drama *Green Grow the Lilacs*, which had served as *Oklahoma!*'s source material. Under the auspices of the Theatre Guild, the play had been a modest success on Broadway in 1931, running a respectable 64 performances. Riggs, who was determined to capture the speech patterns and folk culture of the Southwest in his plays, had based *Lilac*'s characters on members of his family, neighbors, and local figures he had known during his boyhood in Claremore. His play also included 11 folk songs indigenous to the area, sung by cast members in the course of the action or during scene changes by actual rodeo cowboys hired for the occasion; *Green Grow the Lilacs* was not a musical, and yet it was filled with authentic regional music.

After its Broadway run, the play was performed by community theater groups and at colleges through the 1930s, but it wasn't until Hammerstein reworked Riggs's text, and Rodgers added newly written songs, that the story found a wide—or to be more precise, an enormous—audience. Consequently, Riggs occupies a curious position in theater history: Everyone who loves theater knows *Oklahoma!*, yet practically no one, it seems, knows Lynn Riggs.

His name can be found in playbills for *Oklahoma!* whenever it is revived, on cast albums, and in the credits of the movie and video adaptations, but the nature of his contribution is unclear. He did not compose the show's famous songs, nor choreograph its dances. What he did, rather, was recreate the milieu of his hometown, concoct a story, populate it with people he knew, and allow them to express themselves. "I let my characters write their own speeches," Riggs told a reporter from the *New York Post* in 1931, just before *Lilacs* opened. "Whatever poetry may be found in the play is to the credit of my neighbors, not of myself."

BEFORE 'LILACS'

Lynn Riggs wrote 21 full-length dramas, numerous one-act plays, and many poems. He contributed to the screenplays of several movies, and, toward the end of his life, wrote two plays for television. It's fair to say that nothing in his upbringing suggested literature as a potential career path. His people were ranchers, farmers, and businessmen. Singing, dancing, and playacting were regarded as pleasant leisure-time activities, but the notion someone might earn a living doing these things did not seem to occur to anyone else in the Riggs family.

Rollie Lynn Riggs was born in Claremore, Indian Territory, on August 31, 1899, to William and Rose Ella Riggs. Lynn's father was brought to Claremore from Missouri in a covered wagon as a boy. Lynn's mother, who was known as "Eller," was a native of Indian Territory and one-eighth Cherokee. Lynn was the youngest of Eller's five children, two of whom died in infancy. He scarcely knew his mother, who died of typhoid fever when he was two years old. Six months later, William Riggs married a woman named Juliette Chambers, and went on to father two more sons with his second wife. Juliette came to embody the cruel stepmother figure for Lynn and his older brother and sister; she reserved all her maternal affection for her own two boys, and ignored her husband's children by his first wife, except to scold or punish them.

Lynn hated his stepmother but received no sympathy from his father. William Riggs, who worked as a bank official and raised cattle, was a self-centered and emotionally distant man. He showed little interest in the bookish Lynn. When the situation at home grew tense, Lynn would be sent across town to stay with William's sister, Mary Thompson. This was a preferable arrangement for all, for Mary was a good-hearted, gregarious person. She was a divorcée with eight children, mostly girls, and her household was suffused with warmth. When Lynn became gravely ill at age 11 with typhoid fever, it was Aunt Mary, not his stepmother, who nursed him back to health.

Upon graduation from high school in 1917, Lynn got a job as a cattle-puncher, and rode with a herd on a freight train to Chicago. For the next couple of years he lived in various cities and took all kinds of jobs. In New York, he clerked at Macy's, read proof for the *Wall Street*

Journal, and picked up work as a movie extra. Back in Oklahoma, he re-ported for the *Oil and Gas Journal,* and began writing poetry on the side.

Next, he hopped a freight train for Los Angeles and tried unsuc-cessfully to sell a movie scenario to Goldwyn Pictures, then got a job as a proofreader at the *Los Angeles Times.* This was the period of the "Red Scare," when a wave of terrorist bombings erupted in cities across the country. Lynn was present when one such bombing occurred, resulting in several casualties. His eyewitness account of this tragedy, which he sold to the McClure Newspaper Syndicate, earned him $300. He used the money to go to Norman and enroll in the University of Oklahoma as a fine arts major for the fall 1920 semester.

At OU, Lynn studied music and drama and wrote his first play, a one-act called *Cuckoo,* a "folk comedy" with songs. His poems and short stories appeared in campus publications. William Riggs, who by this time was president of a bank in Claremore, contributed no money to his son's education; luckily, Lynn's mother had left her three surviv-ing children land granted her by the Dawes Allotment Act. Lynn was able to mortgage his portion of the land to put himself through college.

Unfortunately, mid-way into his senior year, he was jilted by his girlfriend, suffered a nervous breakdown, and left OU without grad-uating. He went to an artists' colony in Santa Fe to recuperate, and it was there, surrounded by poets and writers in a setting he came to love, that Lynn made a significant personal discovery. Under the benign encouragement of a flamboyant poet named Witter Bynner, Lynn became aware of his homosexual orientation. Unlike Bynner, he would maintain discretion in his personal life, in keeping with the code of silence that prevailed at the time. According to scholar Phyllis Braunlich, whose biography of Riggs is titled *Haunted by Home,* he was freed by the realization of his sexuality but "constantly wary of Oklahoma's judgments." Years later, when Riggs was profiled in the *Southwest Review,* he asked the article's author to omit Bynner's name.

Lynn recovered his health in Santa Fe, and made many friends. At the behest of Ida Rauh Eastman, ex-wife of writer Max Eastman, he focused his efforts on playwriting. Over the next two years, based in Santa Fe, he wrote and staged several dramas, starting with *Knives from Syria,* which concerned a Syrian peddler who sells hard-to-find goods to women in remote Southwestern towns. (The character would return in *Lilacs*.) In 1926 Lynn moved to Chicago, where he taught at the Lewis Institute and wrote a tragedy called *Big Lake*, about an innocent young couple menaced by bootleggers. This play would mark Riggs's Broadway debut in April 1927, and although it was not a success, it brought him attention. His crime drama *The Domino Parlor* was next slated for production, but this project ended badly when Lynn refused to make plot changes demanded by the producers, the powerful Shubert brothers. They closed the show while it was still in previews. The author's resentment would persist.

WRITING 'LILACS'

In the summer of 1928, Riggs became the first Oklahoman to be granted a Guggenheim fellowship. He sailed for Europe, where he lived the life of an ex-pat artist, alongside many of America's best-known literary figures. He saw bullfights in Pamplona and attended the theater in Paris. During the cold winter months, Lynn left Paris for Cagnes-sur-Mer, several miles from Nice, where he began a new play initially titled *Shivaree*. A "shivaree" was a wedding-night folk custom of European origin, common in 19th century America, particularly frontier communities, which involved boisterous mockery of newlyweds by locals.

The play, set in turn-of-the-century Claremore, concerns a young cowboy named Curly McClain and the girl he fancies, an 18-year-old orphan named Laurey Williams, who has been raised by her Aunt Eller. Laurey is attracted to Curly, but disturbed by the attentions of a crude farmhand named Jeeter Fry, who is obsessed with her. Curly and Laurey are wed, but their wedding night shivaree turns into a nightmare: After jeering rowdies force the newlyweds up a ladder to the top of a haystack, Jeeter arrives, drunk, and attempts to set the hay on fire. The two narrowly escape. Jeeter fights Curly, then falls on his own knife, and dies. Curly is arrested, but breaks jail and returns to Laurey. The marshal's men follow, but the couple is permitted to consummate their marriage in privacy, with the understanding that Curly will be taken into custody in the morning.

In writing this play, which would become *Green Grow the Lilacs*, Riggs was motivated to do more than simply tell a story. As he explained in letters to friends, he wished to capture the melodies of

Southwestern speech, "that lustrous imagery, that beautiful rhythmic utterance." He chose not to write about well-educated or privileged folk, but rather "the ones with the most desolate fields, the most dismal skies." He sought to "publish the humanity" of people who did not otherwise receive much attention, and in something resembling their own language. When Riggs wrote poetry he employed a formal, classical style, but when he wrote his Oklahoma plays he tried to channel the language he recalled from childhood:

> AUNT ELLER
> Sing me a song, Curly McClain.
>
> CURLY
> Aw, I cain't sing now! I told you. Not if I tried and tried, and even et cat-gut. And even 'f I drunk the gall of a turkey gobbler's liver, I couldn't sing a-tall.
>
> AUNT ELLER
> Liar and a hypocrite and a shikepoke! Ain't I heared you? Jist now. You sing! Er I'll run you off the place.
>
> CURLY
> I cain't sing, I told you! 'Ceptin' when I'm lonesome. Out in the saddle when it ain't so sunny, er on a dark night close to a fa'r when you feel so lonesome to God you could die . . . Whur you been, anyhow, whose side meat you been eatin' all yer life, not to know nobody cain't sing good 'ceptin' when he's lonesome?

Riggs would identify his Aunt Mary as the model for *Lilacs*' Eller, and one of her daughters—his cousin Laura—as the model for Laurey. A cowboy who worked for the family was the play's Curly, while Jeeter (rechristened Jud in *Oklahoma!*) was based on a farmhand named Jetar Davis, who was recalled by one of Lynn's cousins as a "dirty old boy" and a drunkard.

When Riggs wrote to friends or spoke to journalists about his plays, he never claimed that the dialect he endeavored to preserve was his own; nor was it said that he drawled, or dotted his speech with homey metaphors. He was cultured and well-spoken. In his statements about giving a voice to the Oklahomans of his youth, he referred to "them," not "we" or "us." He seldom returned to Claremore as an adult, and when he did visit he did not tend to linger. Riggs's friend and fellow playwright Paul Green observed that Lynn had an effete, "Parisian" quality, hated gardening and farming, and had "turned away from the Oklahoma environment that he often wrote about." Riggs was an ethnographer among his own people.

STAGING 'LILACS'

In October of 1929, the Theatre Guild agreed to produce *Green Grow the Lilacs*, but for various reasons, the premiere was postponed over a year, until January of 1931. The play's climax was a point of disagreement. Theresa Helburn and her colleagues felt that audiences needed assurance that Curly would be acquitted for the death of Jeeter. Riggs, still pained by his *Domino Parlor* experience, reworked the finale with reluctance, and eventually satisfied all parties. (Meanwhile, he wrote to a friend that if the producers didn't like his revised ending, "they can hang from a sour apple tree.")

Once the script was completed, Helburn saw to it that the play was carefully mounted and properly cast. Franchot Tone starred as Curly, Helen Westley was Aunt Eller, and the role of the peddler was taken by Lee Strasberg, who would become a renowned acting teacher. Latter-day fans of *Oklahoma!* will find noticeable differences between the play and the musical: Ado Annie is little more than a minor character in *Lilacs*, while lariat-twirling Will Parker is mentioned only in passing, never seen. But the tense, emotional triangle comprised of Laurey, Curly, and Jeeter (a.k.a. Jud) is prominent, and extensive passages of Riggs' dialogue between these characters would be retained in the musical, as librettist Oscar Hammerstein readily acknowledged.

Green Grow the Lilacs was greeted with generally positive reviews. Riggs' use of vernacular language was widely applauded, even by critics who were otherwise lukewarm. The predominant response was captured by the *New York Times'* Brooks Atkinson, who admired the playwright's dialogue but felt that he had not fully dramatized the action, concluding that "when Mr. Riggs has learned more about the theater and found a concrete theme he will bring rich material into focus." Despite the economic impact of the Depression, the show played to good houses for several weeks, and after it closed a road company toured the U.S. under Guild auspices.

AFTER 'LILACS'

Riggs' Broadway success brought him offers to write for the movies. In the mid-1930s he lived in Hollywood, wrote screenplays, and rubbed elbows with stars. He became a popular escort for actresses who were divorced or otherwise unattached. Lynn was a witty conversationalist and a good dancer, and as a gay man, he provided their male companionship without complications.

During one period, he escorted Bette Davis to so many events they were assumed (by some) to be romantically involved; a columnist for the *Hollywood Reporter* announced that Riggs and Davis were "ablaze." She was amused, but he was mortified. In 1935, he attended the wedding of Joan Crawford and Franchot Tone, *Lilacs'* original Curly. Crawford became a close friend and gave Lynn a Scotty dog he named The Baron.

Riggs made good money in Hollywood, but he didn't keep it. It was said that when he had money, he spent it, and when he moved back to Santa Fe in the late '30s to refocus his efforts on playwriting, his savings were meager. Two more of his plays made it to Broadway—*Russet Mantle* and *The Cream in the Well*—but neither found great success. He got by on teaching jobs, and then when the war broke out he was drafted into the Army. Riggs was in the Signal Service in Ohio, making training films, when a community theater production of *Lilacs* in Connecticut prompted Theresa Helburn to consider turning the play into a full-fledged musical. She contacted Richard Rodgers, he contacted Oscar Hammerstein, and the rest, as they say, is history.

Riggs was granted leave to attend the Broadway opening of *Oklahoma!* with a friend named Miranda Levy, a clerk at the posh Bergdorf-Good-man department store. According to Levy, he was delighted with the show, and came to the store the next day to buy gifts for everyone in the cast. Privately, however, he told his friend Ida Rauh Eastman that he regretted the loss of *Lilac*'s genuine folk songs. Nonetheless, the musical's spectacular success was a welcome windfall: Over the course of *Oklahoma!*'s five-year run, Riggs earned approximately $2,000 per month in royalties.

At least one critic, Richard Watts of the *New York Herald Tribune*, declared that Riggs did not receive sufficient credit for his contribution to the show. Lynn's attitude is difficult to determine. When the libretto was published by Samuel French, Inc, he complained to the company about the placement of his name on the cover; with friends, however, he joked that the royalty payments had kept his liquor cabinet well-stocked with bourbon.

As he reached his early 50s Riggs, long a heavy smoker, began to struggle with his health. He bought a home on New York's Shelter Island, continued to write, and turned his attention to a novel. *Oklahoma!* supplied him with one more pleasant surprise in 1953 when MGM purchased the movie rights. A neighbor recalled the day when Lynn ripped open an envelope, read the contents, and shouted: "My God, I'm rich! This is $75,000! It's more money than I've ever had in one piece all my life!" Sadly, he didn't have long to spend it. Lynn Riggs died of cancer on June 30, 1954, at the age of 54. He left an unfinished novel, whose plot was based on an unsolved homicide he recalled from his boyhood in Oklahoma. Haunted by home, it seems, to the very end.

Sources for this story include Phyllis Cole Braunlich's Haunted by Home: the life and letters of Lynn Riggs *(Univ. of Oklahoma Press: Norman, 1988); Tim Carter's* Oklahoma!: the making of an American musical *(Yale Univ. Press: New Haven, 2007); Max Wilk's* OK! : the story of "Oklahoma!" *(Applause: New York, 2002); and the clippings files of the Billy Rose Theatre Division, New York Public Library for the Performing Arts.*

THE SOUL OF THE GAME

Soccer is making a comeback in the U.S., and there's a fight brewing in Tulsa for who will be the city's ultimate pro team.

By *RJ Young*

ALL THIS MAN WANTS TO DO RIGHT NOW is find the damn game. It's a Saturday in the middle of the European football calendar, so there's got to be a soccer game on television. There's *got* to be.

He leans across the bar, watching the barkeep click away at the remote, doing her best to satisfy his need to see some of the world's best have a go at each other on a field as long as any Peyton Manning played on but nearly twice as wide. She goes to the TV's guide for help, and finally finds a game.

The channel changer stops on the beIN Sports network. But the screen informs them their package doesn't allow for this channel. They'll have to contact their cable provider if they want to watch the Serie A today.

"Cheap bastards here," Charlie Mitchell says inside Charlie Mitchell's Modern Pub.

Mitchell, the first ever Tulsa Roughneck player, sits cross-armed at a table in front a blind-covered window that makes his white hair seem silver, his skin flush. Now he's telling stories. Old stories. Stories about the enchanting country that raised him, made new by some characteristics that never left him.

"I'm sure you'll pick up my accent," he says.

Of course you do. Just as you pick up his wit, his sense of humor, and his love for a game that has begun to take hold of this nation enamored with balls oblong, balls stitched, and balls bounced. Mitchell, in his 60s now, began playing soccer about the time most folks begin grade school. He grew attached to it because, frankly, there weren't a whole hell of a lot of choices in Paisley, Scotland, a town renowned for weaving and sewing patterns but still big enough to kick *your* ass.

Mitchell could swim or he could play soccer. It wasn't that tough a choice for him, and he didn't mind playing the game from sunup to sundown and twice on Saturday. He'd play for his school team in the morning and his church team in the evening.

The teams didn't change that much either, so he got to know all of the kids he played against and all the dips and dots on that high-cut patch of grass they called a pitch. In the winter, the field was cold and hard. In the summer, when it would rain often, the field was muddy, and Mitchell had to learn how to chip from the kind of lie that would give even Phil Mickelson fits.

Those games were always competitive, and almost no one was substituted on or off. Eleven players would start the game, and if a player got hurt midway through it, his team either played with 10 men or just told the poor injured fella to play close to the touchline.

"You just put them on the wing, and hopefully they could cross the ball every now and again because that was kind of the weakest position," Mitchell says.

Route One[1] football was the philosophy those teams played by for the most part, but some of them grew more sophisticated as their players muscled through puberty with tree trunks for thighs and peach fuzz for mustaches. Mitchell played on one of the better local high school

---

1 Route One football is a singular attack on the defense using long passes—mostly through the air—to earn shots on goal. It's a less glamorous and more physical style of play than the beautiful artistic style some teams, notably Brazil's national team, are famous for.

teams in the land called Camphill High.[2] Back then, scouts didn't neces-sarily go out of their way to find diamonds in the rough. They just went straight to the mines, and Mitchell's team fielded some gems.

Some folks from a local pro team, St. Mirren Football Club, saw Mitchell play, saw his team win, and thought enough of him to offer him an amateur professional contract. They would pay for his kit, boots, and other expenses. Mitchell's contract also put him on the hook for certain chores. He'd be responsible for cleaning the true professionals' boots, painting the railings in the stands of the stadium, and whatever else management thought should go on his honey-do list.

If Mitchell's contract sounds an awful lot like he was going through trade school, that's because he was. The official term for what St. Mir-ren was asking him to become was professional apprentice. At 17 and trying to make a living playing a kids' game, he saw no reason to turn down the deal.

He spent his first year with the Buddies[3] as a youth player, which meant he was on the team behind the reserve team, which was behind the first team. He was third string. Making it to a pro team didn't mean actually making it. There was still work to do. There were still challenges, and this was one of many in his professional soccer career.

A KEEPER KEEPS COMING

Years ago, Sonny Dalesandro forced himself to give up playing pro-fessional soccer. He was older and more realistic than he was in his youth. The time had come to put away a young man's dreams. "It's over, and there's nothing romantic about it," he said. "It's a hard, cold fact of life that I had to deal with. The demons from my playing days, they're always going to be there. There's nothing I can do to make my playing career end any differently than it did."

For a good long while, Dalesandro thought he'd be a player. Don't we all? What glory is there in simply paying the men who win the tro-

---

2 Camphill High School later merged with another school in 1988 to create Gleniffer High.
3 St. Mirren's F.C. two nicknames: Saints and Buddies.

phies? He got serious about trying to go pro after attending Cascia Hall and being on the losing end of a few state championships. He ended up getting drafted by a National Professional Soccer League team in Tampa Bay, which promptly traded his rights to a franchise in Wisconsin called the Milwaukee Wave.

At 19, he was the backup goalkeeper on the squad behind Victor Nogueira, a man many consider to be one of the greatest indoor keepers of all time. On January 31, 1997, Dalesandro saw his first game action for the team in a 21–10 victory against the Toronto Shooting Stars. He bounced around indoor soccer over the next several years. He played against some good players in some nice cities, but never came close to playing for the kind of clubs and in the kind of stadiums he once envisioned. He had his restaurant, Dalesandro's Italian Cuisine, so he didn't have to grind it out as a keeper on mediocre indoor teams. But the thought of never making it ate at him.

He'd carried those thoughts and feelings for 10 years when he traveled north to Wichita to see what the reincarnation of the Wichita Wings, a Major Indoor Soccer League team, looked like. He watched the game, knowing he could still see it well, knowing he could still read it well. He spoke with the Wings' coaches after the game, and they saw no reason why he couldn't help them if he got himself fit. They told him he wouldn't start, but he'd play. That got Dalesandro going.

He worked into shape. He started drilling with a goalkeeper trainer, and he mentally prepared himself for what he thought lay ahead of him—teenage and 20-something kids who are bigger, stronger, faster than he remembered. Then reality set in.[4] His restaurant lost a couple fellas who worked in the kitchen, and he was reminded his restaurant is how he makes his living. How could he leave his business during the week to make training three hours away for a pauper's sum? He couldn't do it, but his competitive nature didn't have to die along with his pro playing career though. And he wasn't going to let it.

Dalesandro kept playing on a men's league team, one he helped start in 2005 called the Boston Avenue Athletic Club, nicknamed the Ath-

---

4 Good thing, too. After two seasons, the Wichita Wings folded following the 2012–13 season—for the second time.

letics. The club was named for a tiny strip of Tulsa where Dalesandro's restaurant is located. Over the years, with Dalesandro's help running the club, it became fairly competitive. It didn't take him long to wonder what he might be able to do if he really went after making a business out of his true passion—soccer. He made some calls.

Now, he's here, past the green and yellow wallpapered front room of the Tulsa Athletics office, decorated with insignia. Walk by a trophy celebrating first place in the South Central Division of the National Premier Soccer League. Glance at the picture frame commemorating a shootout loss before a crowd of 5,788 to Mexico's vaunted Club América, and then stroll down the whitewashed hallway to an office on the right.

His office is the same one where he shot a funny short with former Tulsa Roughnecks Bill Caskey and Victor Moreland, a nod to his marketing savvy and legitimate need to incorporate the forbearers of Tulsa's pro-soccer tradition. Dalesandro sits at his desk with the kind of salt-and-pepper mohawk you saw in Miley Cyrus' "Wrecking Ball" video and Justin Bieber's smiling mug shot. His torso is clad in a blue-and-red plaid shirt with sleeves rolled up just far enough to reveal his tattooed left forearm. The top two buttons are left undone, so a bush of hair can punch from his chest. This ain't your daddy's professional sports owner.

To his right is a game-worn Giorgio Chinaglia jersey,[5] which his former high school coach, Athletics coach Joey Ryan, gave him as a present. A little farther right hangs his 1996 USISL Rookie of the Year plaque, an award he won while playing for a less successful, semi-professional team that was named after the Tulsa Roughnecks and was coached by Moreland, but held none of the panache or style of those early 1980s teams. But there was nothing Dalesandro, a former Cascia Hall goalkeeper, could do about that then. He just wanted to play, wanted to be a part of the Roughnecks.

The original Roughnecks are one of the reasons he's here now as the chairman of the Athletics, trying to make a go of it in a league recognized as fourth-division football in a country where first-division football is played with pads, helmets, and pigskin. Dalesandro and his

---

5 The jersey is the kind of gift that can—and did—bring an NASL-geek like Dalesandro to tears.

partner in his Athletics venture, Dr. Tom Kern, were spoon-fed the Roughnecks as kids.

"We watched that be the catalyst to Tulsa becoming a soccer community," Dalesandro said. "It played a huge part in my life in the sense that I knew I wanted to be around the game."

To join the National Premier Soccer League as an owner, you have to secure a facility that holds at least 500 people and is equipped with locker rooms, a press box, and restrooms. You have to be able to afford the expansion fee. In 2015, that fee will be $12,500—or bit more than you probably paid for your first car. Once the league's members approve your joining the NPSL, you're in. If it seems as simple to buy a franchise in the NPSL as it would be for Einstein to solve a Rubik's Cube, that's because it is designed to be. The NPSL is a non-profit with a mission to grow the sport in a sustainable way. It's a bus league made up of four regions with several conferences based on geography. Most of the teams in the league field squads are made up of mostly amateurs.[6] Before you can build a championship side though, you need a home. Dalesandro finalized the lease on the old Drillers Stadium at 15th Street and Yale Avenue just 41 days before their first home kickoff in 2013, at a price of $5,500 a month. But there was a reason they were willing to shell out that amount of cash for a dilapidated building that had sat mostly vacant for nearly four years.

"We didn't want to play at high school," Dalesandro said. "We wanted to have that professional feel, and even though this isn't a soccer-specific stadium, it's a professional stadium. It has a really great nostalgic feel when you walk through the gates here."

---

6 That's another quirk in the NPSL system. The league is structured so a team can be classified as either professional or amateur. This a necessity for some teams like the Athletics, who field a team comprised mostly of high school and college-age players, particularly from the neighboring University of Tulsa. By classifying themselves as amateur, the Golden Hurricane players who also want to be Athletics don't forfeit their NCAA eligibility.

There was one other reason, too. "Beer. It was paramount to me, especially, that if you're going to a match, you should be able to drink beer. It sounds funny, but the supporters love that. It creates an environment. There's an atmosphere. You can't have beer in high schools, and there's no other stadium in Tulsa where we can sell beer and play soccer. So that, sort of, in a way, handcuffed us to this place."

They built a beer garden and temporary stands in the outfield. They asked local vendors with food trucks to set up in right field—not too far from the Jupiter jumps—and they painted the outfield wall in the green and gold team colors.[7] They set up a fan section for the ultimate Athletics fans[8] and set the general admission price at just $5. Their goal in 2013 was to get as many people through the gates of the baseball stadium to see a soccer game as possible. And it worked.

In their inaugural season, the Athletics averaged nearly 3,300 fans a game.[9] From his office chair, sitting below an Athletics scarf that reads "Tulsa Til I Die," Dalesandro explains the franchise is still only just beginning, only starting to figure out what it's capable of accomplishing. His ambition for the club, though, is lofty. "Our goal here with the Athletics is to bring the MLS to Tulsa," he says.

He wants to do that without riding the coattails of what the original Roughnecks built while paying homage to the men who did the heavy lifting. It's the reason Dalesandro and Kern chose to keep the nickname and crest from the Boston Athletic Club. "To try to re-create what they did by name is to do what they did a disservice," Dalesandro says.

Thing is, his goal has been taken up by a separate group of professional-sports owners downtown. The group has already secured a stadium. It has already bought the rights to a franchise in a league above

---

7 When I asked Dalesandro why he picked green and gold as the team's colors, he said, "Green is for Green Country, and trophies are gold, baby."
8 "Ultras," they're called.
9 For perspective according to the MLS Attendance blog, the worst average attendance during the 2013 MLS regular season was set by Chivas USA at 8,366. The best average attendance for a team belonged to the Seattle Sounders at 44,038.

the NPSL in the U.S. soccer pyramid. Its team will begin play in 2015, and it ain't shy about using the Roughneck name.

AMERICAN FÚTBOL

If Mitchell could display ability and wherewithal, he knew he could work his way up to the St. Mirren first team in time. It didn't take nearly as long as he thought to catch a break, though. By the end of his first year with the club, agents from overseas were beginning to take note of young up-and-comers like him. Players like him would soon make up a new professional soccer league someone had the grand notion to start in America. It called for young fellas like Mitchell and old warhorses with name recognition to fill rosters on teams in Miami, Baltimore, Kansas City, Oakland, and dozens of other cities known more for their football than their football.

One of those agents got ahold of Mitchell and said he could get him a contract in one of three countries on two continents. He had his choice of playing professionally in South Africa, Canada, or the United States. Mitchell couldn't find any fault in playing soccer in the U.S. and signed a deal to play for the Rochester Lancers in Rochester, New York, as a part of the newly formed North American Soccer League.

The league was just two years old then but growing like a brushfire in drought-stricken country. Mitchell was down to ride. In his first season with the Lancers, they won the NASL title, and he was named to the league All-Star team. He'd make four more All-Star teams, earn the captain's armband in Rochester, and appear in 121 games for the Lancers before the biggest club in the NASL came calling in 1976. He made the five-hour trip south to New York City and began playing on the back line of the New York Cosmos.

The Cosmos were the flagship franchise of the league. With players like perhaps the greatest soccer player of all time in Pelé and other world-renowned players like Keith Eddy[10] and Chinaglia on the roster, they'd become must-watch soccer. Folks who'd never shown an interest

---

10 Following the end of his professional career, Eddy founded the Tulsa Soccer Club.

in the game before came out to see the South American and European stars in their element. In 1976, the team averaged more than 18,000 spectators per game at Yankee Stadium, where they played their home games because they'd outgrown Downing Stadium's 22,000-seat capacity. In later years they'd average north of 47,000 fans for regular season games. It was during that '76 season that Mitchell put his stamp on the league in a game against the Miami Toros—with a bit of help from one of the game's greatest players.

Mitchell was sprinting down the touchline on an overlap toward the right corner flag of the opposing goal in the house that Ruth built when he received a cross from the other side. He took a soft first touch to give himself space, and then lifted the ball into the 18-yard box. Then he looked up. Pelé was mid-somersault and throwing his right foot at the ball. It crashed into the back of the net. The sequence made ABC's *Wide World of Sports*.

Folks of a certain age remember that bicycle kick. Mitchell recollects Pelé's gesture when the final whistle blew. "I'll always remember after the game was over he gave me his shirt," Mitchell says. "He said, 'Tell your grandchildren about this, Charlie, because that's the first bicycle kick I've scored in the United States.' "

That was the highlight of a short stay with the Cosmos for Mitchell. He seldom saw playing time in New York City. After playing no fewer than 14 games in any season with the Lancers, he'd played just seven total with the Cosmos. He was just 28 years old then, and he wanted to play. He asked to be traded.

It didn't take long for folks to show interest. One of them was Hubert Vogelsinger. Vogelsinger offered Mitchell a chance to play with a new franchise he was coaching called Team Hawaii. Mitchell made for the islands.

––––––––––

Team Hawaii was built on the ashes of the San Antonio Thunder. After two seasons in the NASL, the Thunder had drawn just a little more than 5,000 fans per game. Soccer hadn't taken hold of Texas quite yet. The club's owner, Ward Lay Jr., wanted to see if he could still get his money's worth out of the franchise. After all, who wouldn't want to play in Hawaii?

The team was good, making the playoffs in its only year in the NASL, even after Vogelsinger was sacked with 10 games left in the season. Mitchell was promoted to player-manager and guided Team Hawaii to the playoffs. Along the way he marked truly great players like George Best and beat him. Or, at least Team Hawaii did.

After dropping a game on April 17, 1977, to Best's Los Angeles Aztecs 6 – 0, Team Hawaii got one back with a 6 – 5 win on July 22, 1977, in Honolulu. The sixth goal was scored in extra time.

Unlike most fledgling clubs, winning more than they it lost wasn't the problem for Team Hawaii. Getting folks to play in Honolulu wasn't a problem either. Getting folks to watch the team play was something else entirely—on top of Team Hawaii's travel predicament. It wasn't un-common for the team to play five consecutive away games for logistical reasons. Frequently, teams would only fly to Honolulu after playing against at least one other left-coast opponent. After just one season on the island, Lay had had enough. He put the team up for sale. The cities that emerged as the frontrunners for the franchise were Milwaukee, Cleveland, and Tulsa.

A NEW GAME IN TOWN

The headline in the *Tulsa World* read, "Pro Soccer headed to ONE-OK Field in 2015." The art for sportswriter Mike Brown's story in the December 19, 2013, edition of the broadsheet showed Tulsa Drillers general manager Mike Melega in a blue suit and red tie holding up a red scarf like a triumphant Liverpool fan following a lopsided win in the Merseyside Derby.

But it wasn't a win over a hated rival he was celebrating. It was the Drillers' purchase of a professional United Soccer Leagues Pro team. The scarf read USL PRO TULSA 2015, which is as succinct as it is non-descript. The story was placed above the fold, above a story about an Oklahoma Sooner wide receiver who would soon lead his team to Sugar Bowl glory—so you know it was important.

A little over a month after the story was published, I walked inside the $39.2 million downtown complex built for a Double-A ball club and could practically smell the new money. Unlike the Athletics' setup, there's a stately secretary on the lower level of the first floor to greet me. Her first order of business is to ascertain *my* order of business. Duly satisfied, she asked me to sit and wait, giving me time to examine the wood floor, the flat screen TV, copies of *Sports Illustrated* on the table, cushioned chairs in front of the executive entrance, and the red USL PRO TULSA 2015 scarf adorning the back of her chair.

It's not long before Melega bursts through an entrance to take me toward the elevator that leads to the Drillers front office. On the ride up, I can't help but notice the two fliers framed near the switches. One advertises the cost of a business suite for the upcoming baseball season. The other shows the rewards for a $25 season ticket deposit for USL PRO soccer in Tulsa—next year. Once on the office floor, I stroll the hallway with Melega, stopping to pick up Drillers director of media and public relations, Brian Carroll, before taking a seat in Melega's office.[11] Melega didn't come up a soccer fan. Baseball raised him, and baseball pays him. So why are he and his bosses, Drillers co-chairmen Dale and Jeff Hubbard, getting into the football business? Well, Melega saw an old friend, John Allgood, getting into the soccer business out west[12] and called him to see what the fuss was about. Besides being a baseball man,[13] Allgood is a person with a long title.

He's the senior executive vice president for business development for Oklahoma City's minor league hockey team, the Barons. The Barons are owned by Prodigal LLC, an event management company in Oklahoma City. On July 2, 2013, Prodigal's CEO, Bob Funk Jr., formally announced Prodigal had secured a USL PRO franchise for Oklahoma City. The franchise, now called the Oklahoma City Energy Football Club, or Energy FC, began its inaugural season in April. While landing a USL PRO squad for Oklahoma City, Prodigal secured the rights to a franchise in Tulsa, too. It can cost between $75,000 and $750,000 to purchase a USL franchise depending on which of the leagues an own-

---

11 A space bigger than my first apartment.
12 i.e. Oklahoma City.
13 Allgood is the former executive director of the Oklahoma City Redhawks.

ership group wishes to join. For a USL PRO franchise, USL's top league, the operating budget can be upward of $3 million.

There's reason for a USL PRO team to cost more than an NPSL team. Though each is considered a developmental league in the U.S. soccer pyramid, USL PRO stands one rung higher than NPSL. USL PRO also recently formed an agreement with MLS that ensures MLS franchises will either enlist a USL PRO team as an affiliate or create its own USL PRO team in place of an affiliation with an existing one.

The affiliation? An exchange of players that is similar to baseball's minor league system. Energy FC has already formed an affiliation with MLS's Sporting Kansas City. There's more. USL PRO teams don't have to remain in the USL, and, for that matter, neither do NPSL teams. But USL PRO teams have a track record for joining the ranks of the MLS, especially lately.

Last November Orlando City Soccer Club became the 21st club to join MLS after just three years in USL PRO. The team begins play in America's top flight in 2015, year 20 of the MLS. English footballer and all-around hunk David Beckham recently exercised the option in his MLS player contract to purchase an MLS franchise. He plans to locate it in Miami, Florida, at the bargain price expansion fee price of $25 million. MLS commissioner Don Garber has said he believes there will be 24 teams in the league by 2020.

There's been at least one prominent case of an MLS team playing in a baseball stadium as a USL franchise: The Portland Timbers. The Timbers began as an NASL franchise in 1975. But, like the original Roughnecks, the Timbers folded just a few years before the league did in 1982. Then, in 1985, a group revived the club as an independent with a selection of amateur and pro players in various leagues, until it folded again in 1990. It was resurrected once more in 2001, and, after playing in the A-League and then the USL First Division, the Timbers got the call from Garber and MLS.

The Timbers recently shared PGE Park with the Portland Beavers, a Triple-A baseball club, as well as the Portland State Viking football team. When the city was awarded an MLS franchise in 2009, the Portland City Council voted to kick the baseball club out so renovations could be made to make the facility more soccer specific, though the Portland State football team still plays home games there. They also renamed the place Providence Park. This year, Providence Park will host the 2014 MLS All-Star game. But the Portland Beavers[14] are no more.

When Prodigal learned through Melega that the Drillers were interested in becoming the majority owner of the Tulsa franchise, the Drillers' management was excited. Tulsa would become a natural soccer rival for Prodigal's newest sports venture, and there hasn't been a pro sports turnpike rivalry since the Oklahoma City Blazers and Tulsa Oilers were both in the Central Hockey League.[15] It made sense for both parties to partner. The Drillers own the majority of the team while Prodigal still owns a minority share.

"We've got this beautiful venue," Melega said. "If pro soccer's going to return to Tulsa, it's probably going to have its best chance to succeed in downtown Tulsa at a state-of-the-art venue like we have at ONEOK Field. We have a fantastic front-office staff, so we feel like it's good for the city. It's good to bring more bodies to downtown Tulsa, and it's a great opportunity for the city to perhaps get back on the radar of MLS for future expansion opportunities as well."

At the time, there was still the issue of the team's name though. They had to secure the coveted Tulsa Roughnecks name, right? Turns out, it wasn't so coveted. And the Drillers didn't secure it.

According to the U.S. Patent and Trademark Office, the name "Tulsa Roughnecks" has been filed for five times and had lain abandoned for seven years when Prodigal Soccer LLC applied for the rights to "Tulsa Roughnecks FC" on September 19, 2013. Following the Drillers announcement, they enlisted the city to help vote on what the team should be called.

The finalists on the ballot were Tulsa Roughnecks FC, Tulsa Strike, FC Tulsa, and Oil City FC. The Drillers had applied for the other three

---

14 The Portland Beavers moved to Arizona to become the Tuscon Padres in 2011. In April 2014, the franchise relocated.
15 The Blazers folded in 2009. The Barons play in the American Hockey League. The Oilers play in the Central Hockey League.

names under its soccer business name, Tulsa Professional Soccer LLC, two weeks before the Tulsa Roughnecks FC name won almost 50 percent of the vote. Even before the finalists were announced, Melega lauded Prodigal for protecting the name. "I think that was probably a good move by their people and a forward-thinking idea when they had secured franchise rights for Oklahoma City and Tulsa," he said. Tulsa loves its roughnecks—soccer and otherwise.

THE SIGNATURE WIN

Lay Jr., a Texas man, moved his Team Hawaii franchise for the third time. This time he settled it in Tulsa and renamed it after the slob-ber-knocking, tool-pushing roustabouts who made up the backbone of the town that folks used to call the Oil Capital of the World. Then he hired a coach. The first man charged with making the Tulsa Roughnecks into a winning football club in 1978 was Bill Foulkes.

Foulkes' first order of business in Tulsa was making sure Mitchell didn't go playing—or managing—for anybody else. He sat Mitchell down and told how much he admired him, how he loved the way he went about his business on the pitch, and asked if he wouldn't mind becoming his player-assistant coach? "It was an honor for me to be an assistant player-coach to Bill Foulkes," Mitchell said.

He was the only player on the Team Hawaii roster Foulkes kept. The Roughnecks finished their inaugural season 15 – 15, though, and lost in the first round of the playoffs. For his efforts, Foulkes was canned after his only season in Tulsa. Alan Hinton was brought in to replace him.

Hinton told Mitchell he wanted to keep him, but when Eddy offered Mitchell a job as a player-coach for another franchise in Toronto, Mitch-ell decided he could stand the cold after all. He signed on to play for Eddy and the Toronto Blizzard. That seemed to be the end of Mitchell's career in Tulsa.

Mitchell played every minute of every game the Blizzard played in 1979. However, the Blizzard didn't perform much better than Mitchell's last team. The Blizzard lost more games (16) than it won (14) that year, but made it all the way to the quarterfinals of the NASL playoffs before bowing out to the Cosmos.

Mitchell was 32 years old. He had played for a decade in the NASL and was thinking of moving back to Tulsa, where he still owned a house.

"I always thought I'd come back and retire in Tulsa, retire from soccer," he said. "I like the town. I like the standard of living." So when Roughnecks general manager Noel Lemon[16] called Mitchell to tell him he was no longer happy with Hinton and asked would Mitchell like to manage the team, he was happier than Marie Antoinette in a TastyKake factory.

He took the bench in Tulsa as a full-fledged manager—no more player-coach—for the 1979–80 indoor season and 1980 outdoor season. Later that year, Mitchell and the Roughnecks put the first of a few lasting marks on the city many of them would come to call home.

———

They had to put extra bleachers around Skelly Stadium—what you now know as H.A. Chapman Stadium—at the University of Tulsa's campus to fit all the folks who'd bought tickets. The word was out.

On April 26, 1980, the Roughnecks played host to the NASL's premier team, the Cosmos, and more than 30,000 folks wanted a ticket. The Cosmos were still a club full of world-famous players.[17] Players like Chinaglia, Carlos Alberto, and Franz Beckenbauer. Like Vladislav Bogicevic and Julio Cesar Romero. Oscar Bernardi and Johan Neeskens. They were all in Tulsa, and they'd come to win. "You don't block those guys out," Moreland said. "You can block everything else out, but you have to concentrate on those players. It was every kid's dream to play against those guys."

Mitchell knew Cosmos acting manager and technical director, Julio Mazzei, had a great tea, that the Cosmos had taken four out of five from the Roughnecks, and that the Roughnecks hadn't beaten the Cosmos in three years. He also knew the stars Mazzei had traveled west with were

---

16 Lemon said around the time he hired Mitchell, "We've only been in the league two and a half years and already half the teams hate us. Give me another two years and we'll have them all."

17 That Cosmos team was so good that the NASL pitted an NASL Select team against it on September 24, 1980.

past their primes, while Mitchell had young and hungry fellas with everything to prove playing for him. He wanted to use that.

The Roughnecks were made up of Americans, Germans, Northern Irishmen, Englishmen, and Scots whose idea of football bordered on Barry Swizter's. Mitchell told his team to go on the attack. Make the game as tough and hard as possible—play Roughneck football. And so they did. The Roughnecks led the league in fouls per game heading into the contest and reveled in their physicality against the twinkle-toed Cosmos. The referee that day, Dante Maglio, called 59 fouls and doled out five yellow cards during the game. Early on, it didn't seem to matter. Chinaglia found the net with his 99th goal of the season just 24 minutes in. The Cosmos led 1 – 0 at halftime.

Then, in the 62nd minute, one of Tulsa's emigrated sons, Moreland, knocked a corner kick from Alan Woodward into the back of the net. Tie game. All of a sudden, the Roughnecks were not only in the game but had a chance to win. They only needed one more good opportunity to complete the dream, and it came when Caskey came free and dribbled into a one-on-one showdown with Cosmos keeper Hubert Birkenmeier. Caskey put the go-ahead goal in the back of the onion bag in the 79th minute. The crowd began to celebrate the win—just too early.

"So with 10 minutes in the game, people were coming up to me clapping," Mitchell said. "I'm on the bench, and everybody's going, 'Oh, man! We're going to beat the Cosmos!' And I had to keep telling people, 'This is the Cosmos. The game's not over yet.' Seriously, it was the longest 10 minutes of my life."

Knowing Beckenbauer and Chinaglia alone could score three goals in 10 minutes, Mitchell implored his players to keep possession, to not let the Cosmos anywhere near ball. His Roughnecks held firm and rode out a 2 – 1 victory. The headline in the next day's *Tulsa World* read "Rufnex Forced Cosmos Out of Their Orbit."

"They're not used to playing from behind," Roughneck Jo Edvaldsson told the *World*. "They have seven or eight superstars out there. But we have a team of players who care about each other. You didn't see them going after tackles. We have more character. We deserved to win it."

"It was definitely the greatest game I ever coached," Mitchell says. "Or they ever played."

Mitchell didn't make it past the 1981 season after the Roughnecks finished 15 – 17 in 1980, but he'd laid the groundwork for what was to come. The assistant coach he hired, Terry Hennessy,[18] took over the team and guided it to the first winning season (17 – 15) in franchise history. Two years later, Hennessy led the Roughnecks to their first and only league championship in the 1983 Soccer Bowl with a 2 – 0 win against the Blizzard. The team folded the following year.

The '83 Soccer Bowl remains Tulsa's crowning pro soccer achievement, an achievement the Athletics and Roughnecks FC are chasing. But they'll need more than trophies to bring a major-league sports franchise to Tulsa, and MLS might be the city's last chance to make that dream happen. Today, with MLS becoming big business and the popularity of soccer growing with each year, a fight is brewing for the soccer soul of Tulsa.

---

18 Hennessy was in his second stint as a Roughneck assistant. He had coached the team in 1978.

WILD LIFE

An inside view of furry fandom and the people who blur the line between human and animal.

By *Jezy J. Gray*

THE ROCK FORMATIONS that spill out from the wooded foothills of the Sans Bois Mountains in southeastern Oklahoma were once a draw for outlaws and outcasts. Legend has it that these rocky cliffs and canyons served as a refuge for a number of *personae non gratae*, from Civil War deserters to infamous outlaws like Jesse James, Belle Starr, and the Dalton Gang. The area was incorporated in 1933 by the Civilian Conservation Corps, and four years later it was named Robbers Cave State Park—a nod to its history as a hideout.

Each spring for the past five years, though, Robbers Cave has been a sanctuary for outcasts of a different stripe.

It's 8 a.m. on a Saturday, and after navigating a winding dirt road marked "private," I pull in to Group Camp #2. Parking is scarce at the top of the hill, but I find a spot next to a late-'80s Buick LeSabre whose rear dash is stacked to the ceiling with plush foxes. Idling across the way is a muscular blue Dodge Ram pickup with shoe polish paw prints splashed across the back windows. Beneath that, in block letters: "*Wild Nights 2014! Honk 4 Furries!*"

For the uninitiated, "furry" is shorthand for an enthusiast of the anthropomorphic arts. This is often—but not always—expressed by wearing a "fursuit" depicting a unique animal character, or "fursona," dreamed up by the wearer. The Missouri Exotic Species Arts Association (MESA) held its first annual outdoor furry fandom convention at Robbers Cave in 2009.

It's day three of this year's convention—"*the* day," MESA President Joel Ricketts assured me—and the campsite feels lived in. Tents crouch haphazardly around the perimeter, surrounded by a fortress of slim, towering pine trees. A trailhead on the north end leads past the group cabins and up to Robbers Cave, where tonight's hike will take place. The late-April sky is clear and brilliant, showing no evidence of the severe weather expected overnight.

Despite the relatively early hour, the southern end of the camp is buzzing with activity. I take notice of license plates as I walk toward the crowd. Some are from as far away as California and Maine, but most have come from Oklahoma, Texas, Missouri, Kansas, and Arkansas.

I stop to marvel at a massive and expensive-looking RV wrapped in elaborate wolf-themed artwork. A neon green fursuit hangs from the cab's extended canopy, turning languidly in the morning breeze. Next is a red Ford Ranger with a matching red bumper sticker emphatically announcing that the driver is "*NOT A LIBERAL.*"

One camper nods as he jaunts past, blasting the Bloodhound Gang's raunchy late-'90s novelty hit, "The Bad Touch," from a de-vice attached to his belt loop. "You and me baby ain't nothin' but mammals / so let's do it like they do on the Discovery Channel." I would hear the song at least three more times during the course of my stay.

Small groups socialize at the south-end picnic tables, swapping off-color jokes and chattering about *Dr. Who*. No one is wearing a fur-suit, aside from the occasional pair of plush ears or bushy tail. I'll learn later that it's much more common to see people wearing these animal accents, or "partials," rather than full-body suits, which can cost thou-sands of dollars.

A young man in his early 20s eyes the crowd from the pavilion, his thin frame lost in a homemade Robin Hood costume. His perky auburn fox tail swishes in the wind as he pulls a foam arrow from his quiver and launches it into the crowd. To everyone's delight, a large, bearded man erupts from his folding chair and playfully chases Robin Hood around the camp latrine and down the trail into the woods.

As I'm taking in the scene, I nearly walk into a young couple attached at the throat by flimsy chain-link, making out enthusiastically in the grass. They don't look up as I pass on my way to the mess hall. I approach the wooden double doors ("REGISTER HERE") and pause for a beat, unsure of what's on the other side.

I push them open and walk into the near-capacity mess hall. Here, artists display and sell sketches of anthropomorphic animal characters—some wearing diapers, some sporting '80s punk rock hairstyles—labeled with names like Dracian, davie_x, and Redwulf. Other vendors sell crafted materials and jewelry. There's even a masseuse set up in the corner near the front door, working the shoulders of a partially suited camper whose fuzzy, chocolate brown ears peek out from the cream-colored linen face cradle.

I find Ricketts at the other end of the room next to the registration booth with his brow furrowed purposefully over a clipboard. He's wearing fingerless black gloves, a black t-shirt, black slacks, black non-slip tennis shoes, and a brown leather shark's tooth necklace. His hair is thinning up front but a long, ash-blond mane spills down the back. There's an intense quality about him, which I imagine is amplified by the stress of running such a packed event.

I introduce myself. He suggests a walk-and-talk, saying he's needed at the archery range. This is how most of our interactions would take place, striding purposefully in conversation across camp like two characters in an expository scene from a bizarre episode of *The West Wing*.

"Some furs just got back from horseback riding in the cave," he tells me. "Archery is the next outdoor event, then thrown weapons. We'll do a chili lunch at 11:00, with a couple hours to mingle before fursuit games. Dinner is at 6:00, then boffer-weapons fighting and a drum circle in the evening, before the midnight howl."

———————

I stumbled upon the furry convention by way of a cryptic event page, *Wild Nights in Robbers Cave*, while researching for a camping trip last year. I was soon through the looking glass, puzzled by footage of anthropomorphic foxes, wolves, and tigers parading gleefully through nearby downtown Wilburton (population 2,843). They waved at gawking motorists and mugged for the camera, drunk on their own spectacle. Deeper in, I found photo galleries of furries riding horseback, practicing archery, and dancing with abandon under high-beam strobe lights.

What, exactly, was going on in Robbers Cave, and why had I never heard about it?

It turns out that Wild Nights has been happening here annually for five years. In 2009, it peeled off from yet another outdoor Oklahoma furry convention held four hours west in Roman Nose State Park. This other gathering—called OklaCon—has been going on for a decade, and it's the largest furry campout in the world. Attendance at both is steadily rising, with each convention reporting recent attendance of 300-plus, making Oklahoma the premier destination for furries with a woodsy streak.[1]

This all struck me as too delightfully odd not to investigate.

After months of deliberating, Joel Ricketts—who, in addition to being MESA president, is also Wild Nights' logistics coordinator—agreed to let me camp with the group and write about the event. After making my case to Joel, the issue was brought to a vote at the March 2 meeting of the Wild Nights organizing committee. The next morning, I was a registered attendee.

It wasn't an easy sell. The fandom has historically been painted by the media as deviant and, in the case of a particularly damaging 2003 episode of *CSI*, dangerous.[2] As a result, these conventions tend to be closed events. "My concern," Ricketts told me over the phone, "is that

---

1 According to WikiFur, a collaborative web application created by a young Wild Nights camper from the U.K., there are 19 annual furry campouts in the world. Ontario's "Camp Feral," started in 1998, is the oldest. There are four others in the U.S.—in Kansas, Colorado, Oregon, and Pennsylvania—but their numbers don't come close to Wild Nights and OklaCon. Attendance at most of these other events hovers between 30 and 40, whereas attendance at the twin Oklahoma conventions has been steadily rising through triple digits for years.

2 In the season four episode "Fur and Loathing," forensic evidence leads investigators to a hedonistic furry convention characterized by hard drug use and kinky sex. Ricketts acknowledges the impact the episode has had on popular opinion regarding the fandom, and he says he can understand why: "I watched that episode, and it freaked me out."

other attendees will feel uncomfortable with a member of the media hanging around, given our group's history with the press. We've had a rough go of it in the past, as you may know, and we want to be careful."

I told Ricketts I wasn't particularly interested in the story "Weirdos Dress in Costumes, Have Sex with Each Other." I didn't know what the story was. To find out, I had to go camping.

———

"This is your first fur-con, huh?" A woman, the only one in a group of five, asks. They're lounging in lawn chairs outside of a large tent, puffing e-cigarettes, and watching the archers in the meadow. She says she can tell I'm a first-timer because of my tucked-in flannel shirt. "Plus the boots," she adds, like I know what that means.

She introduces herself as Holly Fox. She's friendly. The whole group is, really. There's PhatCat, a homebrewer from Austin who chats enthusiastically about a beer tasting happening in one of the cabins later that night. Another, called Ipaquey, encourages me to shoot archery with him later, once the crowd thins out.

This is how I meet Allen, an 18-year-old from Grand Prairie, Texas, who self-identifies as a rainbow-colored anthropomorphic fox named Candie Foxalure. He's wearing a tie-dyed do-rag, blue jeans, and a too-large purple t-shirt that says "I'd Cuddle That." His frame is slight, his head shaved, and he maintains eye contact as he introduces himself.

I reach out for a handshake and his face falls with disappointment. Doe-eyed, his bottom lip protruding for effect, he spreads his arms wide. "You don't hug?"

We embrace, in what would be the first of the day's many hugs from strangers.

He's been awake for 20 minutes, and he's already anxious to "suit up." He asks if I want to meet Candie—I do—and delightedly scampers off to change. Despite the skittishness I was warned about, I'm beginning to suspect that I will find no shortage of people eager to talk to me. Everyone wants to enhance my experience. Everyone wants to tell their story.

Allen is what's called a therian. This means that he and his fursona are connected—as he puts it—"mind, body, and soul."

For some, fursuiting is a sort of "cosplay" not unlike what goes on at popular anime and comic conventions. Like those con attendees who role play in elaborate costumes based on characters from video games, comic books, and various pieces of popular culture, some furries see fursuiting as a method of escape and play: a fantasy. For people like Allen, though, it's a core feature of their inner worlds.

He marches back to camp, covered head to toe in a vivid rainbow of fur, with an oversized fox head tucked under his armpit. Before I can comment on his suit, he asks, "Do you want to take some pictures of me in the woods?"

Since I didn't come this far not to follow an anthropomorphic fox into the woods, I say yes. (This would become my mantra for the day: *Say yes, unless it's too creepy.*)

We begin our shoot in a clearing down-trail from the campsite. Right away, it's clear there's no need to direct him for the camera. He launches into a series of playful poses. First he turns away, whipping his neon snout back toward the camera. "I'm a silly fox," he announces, and darts across the clearing.

I feel a little silly myself, kneeling in front of a teenage therian, snapping pictures as he twirls, gallops, and prances in the Oklahoma sunshine.

This goes on for a few more minutes, before it becomes clear that I'll have to be the one to end our session. "I think we got it," I say. He gives me his email address and asks that I send him the pictures.

On our walk back, I learn that Allen is a devoted Christian. I began to pick up on this earlier, as he swatted at a wasp buzzing around his ear. "I hate wasps," he grumbled. Then he stopped mid-stride, steadied himself, and looked plaintively toward the sky. "I'm sorry, God. I *dislike* wasps."

I'm not sure why, but I'm a little taken aback by this. I ask how he sees his faith interacting with his life in the fandom. He says that he feels closest to God when he is wearing his fursuit.

"Ever since I was little, I knew I was a fox. I knew I wasn't really human." He tells me that looking in the mirror was a painful experience for him from a young age. The human reflection was at odds with how he felt inside.

He reconciles this dissonance with a reflection on his faith. "When I die," he tells me, his voice serious and proud, "I truly believe I'll go to heaven as Candie Foxalure."

———————

Allen isn't alone. According to findings published by the Anthropomorphic Research Project, a 2013 survey conducted by the University of Waterloo found that approximately 8 percent of an 800-person sample identified as therians.

The word "therianthropy" arrives in English from the Greek *therion* (wild animal) and *anthrōpos* (human being). Enthusiasts point to its long mythological history throughout the world, and more than one Wild Nights camper references the Navajo "skinwalker" myth: *yee naaldlooshii* ("with it, he goes on all fours").

"I mean, would the people who call us weird say that about the Egyptians for worshipping cats?" This from a camper dressed as an anthropomorphic wolf wearing a Kevin Durant jersey. I couldn't hear him particularly well through the mask, but I didn't feel comfortable asking him to take it off. "You look at history, and the stuff produced by these different cultures—especially different Native American tribes—all have an element of anthropomorphism. Some of us see ourselves continuing this tradition."

Hopi and Mohawk mythologies have their own versions of the skinwalker, as does Norse folklore tradition, where warriors could be transformed by donning a "bear shirt" (*berserkr*) or "wolf coat" (*ulfheðnar*). But as this bright, friendly camper is trying to situate the group in history, I can't help but notice his human stare behind the wolf mask. Most suits have plaster eye pieces with exaggerated pupils, but his only has two holes revealing his hazel green eyes and the slightest tug of age near the corners of their sockets. There is something uncanny and unsettling about this, and it brings to mind something I don't say out loud: In all these folk traditions, the skinwalker is a figure of danger.

We're soon joined by another self-described therian, pushing into his mid-60s, whose identity—like Allen's—is fused with his fursona. He is not in character at the moment due to the heat. "When it's not so hot," he says, "I suit everywhere: at the doctor, the dentist, my real estate agent's office." His fursona is GreyHare, a rabbit that transforms into a wolf. ("I'm a shape-shifter," he tells me. "One of only a few in the whole country.") In human form, he works for the City of Dallas and asked that I not give his name.

"And you might not believe this," GreyHare adds, "but the rabbit has healing powers." He watches me for a moment to gauge my reaction, making sure I'm sufficiently titillated. "That's right. Before I started suiting every day, I was deep in stage-three kidney failure. Since then, I've increased my kidney function by 4 percent and my mobility has improved significantly."

Tenderly, he adds: "The doctors said I should expect to lose function of my legs, but here I am, in Oklahoma, talking to you on this beautiful day. And it's all because of the rabbit."

––––––––––––––

"The fandom is made up of people who've been outcasts most of their lives," Ricketts tells me on the hike to Robbers Cave that evening. "They were the unpopular kids in school. That's a story that recurs over and over again. When we came up in school, it was miserable. It was hell. We were the kids who were constantly teased and picked on."

It's a problem that still persists. While I met people in Wilburton who tolerated the furries—"They don't bother anybody, far as I know," a cattle farmer told me at the Corner Cafe—other locals haven't been as understanding. Last year, a truck full of young guys drove up in the middle of the night and sprayed the camp with paintballs. The year before, a man entered the grounds on foot and verbally harassed campers.

Incidents like these are why the furries no longer parade through downtown Wilburton. As an added precaution, attendees are encouraged to leave their fursuits at camp if they decide to venture into town on their own. "The merchants were all very receptive to us," Ricketts said, "but apparently some people started complaining to the parks department, saying they didn't feel comfortable with us wearing suits in town." That, coupled with these uglier clashes with locals, prompted organizers to turn down the volume on this growing convention's public presence.

Still, Ricketts chalks much of Wild Nights' success up to "Oklahoma hospitality."

MESA initially wanted to hold the event in Missouri, but Ricketts says that they couldn't find a park to take them on. "After seeing our website," he said, "they all started looking for reasons to deny us."

Since OklaCon was already established, MESA was more optimistic about their chances in Oklahoma. "Robbers Cave was most willing to work with us," he said. "The staff has just been phenomenal, and the park itself, as you can see, is just breathtaking."

We're standing on top of the cave, overlooking a spectacular vista of short-leaf pine trees that billow out into gentle, rolling hilltops. Ricketts—a.k.a. Heros, the Noisy Panther—shades his eyes and squints toward the horizon. A cool breeze travels up through the rocks as the setting sun breaks like an egg over the Sans Bois Mountains.

"I'll never forget the first time I hiked this," he tells me. "I came up here alone, the day before our first event in 2009. I got to this plateau above the rocks, right here, and I could see the group camp down below. It was kind of an emotional thing for me." He begins another thought, then shrugs in explanation. "That was it," he says. "That was the moment. I knew we were home."

TWO

REFLECTIONS ON LIFE
IN OKLAHOMA

BOYS WILL BE BOYS

What it's like to grow up gay in small town Oklahoma.

By *John Paul Brammer*

Mr. Smith was an old-fashioned cowboy. He wore tight Wranglers with a circle burned into the back pocket where he kept his snuff, and a big, shiny buckle on his belt. He was rarely seen without his hat and boots. His hat was usually white because he was a good guy.

Mr. Smith was my math teacher at Cache Middle School. I had him in the class right before lunch.

Cache, if you've never heard of it, is a small town not too far from Lawton. A single road runs through it. Its heyday has long gone, but you can still see the bones of old-fashioned ice cream shops, arcades, and pizza parlors—all shut down since Lord knows when.

Every day after Mr. Smith's class, my classmates and I would head over to the high school cafeteria. We'd walk all the way past the old gym that looked like a rusty half-buried aluminum can in the ground. Eighth-graders got to eat with the big dogs.

But one day, I stayed behind in Mr. Smith's classroom.

I stayed because I remembered a story he'd told us on the first day of class.

"I remember there was a group of kids pickin' on a guy," he'd said in his grizzly country accent. "They got to pushin' him around and all that. Well, one of the boys in the group stepped up and stopped 'em.

You know what he said? Said, *'Hey! You leave him alone!'* You know who that boy was?" He'd pointed at himself with his thumb. "That boy was *me*."

"Hey faggot," the familiar voice said cheerfully. "Where ya goin'?"

I didn't say anything. I just kept my head down and kept walking. That was my strategy for survival. Just ignore them until they go away.

Justin was a big, husky guy. Corn-fed, they call it. He was a farmer's son with broad shoulders, rosy, chubby cheeks, and hands like baseball mitts. Ric was a tall, slender kid. He wore the same John Deere shirt most days. People thought of him as the class clown. London was short and blond with a permanent grin on his face. He was from the city and clearly eager to attach himself to a group.

That's the thing about small towns. If you're new, good luck.

"What's wrong faggot?" Ric asked while the big guy gave my chest a hard squeeze. The little one was laughing somewhere behind them. "Why don't you want to talk to us? Aren't we your friends? Huh? Don't you want to be our friend?"

Starting around February, they waited for me every day outside of Mr. Smith's classroom when I left to go to lunch. They'd put their arms around me, holding on to me just tight enough so that I couldn't get away.

"What's up faggot? Did you miss us?"

I never said a word back to them, even though my heart was pounding out of my chest. I kept my head down and walked on the sidewalk to the cafeteria, pretending, as best I could, that their arms weren't hanging around my neck like a noose.

Justin hit me across the face with a hot dog wiener. It felt cold and wet on my cheek. I stared down into my lunch tray and acted like it hadn't happened. There were three of them and only one of me.

"Do you like that?" He asked. "Huh? No? I thought you liked wieners. Don't you like wieners, faggot?"

No matter what they said to me, they never left that word out. Not once. It had caught on with the rest of the kids and had become my name in school.

"What are you doing faggot? Where are you going faggot? What's the matter faggot?"

I became so desensitized to it that whenever someone said my real name it surprised me.

A teacher saw me get hit with the hot dog, but she didn't say anything. None of them ever did. Some of them thought I deserved what I was getting.

Ms. Neal, my reading teacher, had told another class that "if I was going to be weird" then I should come to expect that sort of thing. I know she said that. Some of my classmates who had her were giddy to tell me she'd said it.

London pushed my books down in front of the Spanish teacher one time.

"You guys quit that," she'd said, almost jokingly. She really liked those kids. She had them in class.

———————

I clutched my books tight to my chest as I walked to Mr. Smith's desk. He was grading papers.

"Mr. Smith?" I said quietly.

He looked up at me.

"W'atcha need?" he said.

"They're waiting for me," I said even more quietly.

"Do what now?" he said.

Mr. Smith was a good guy. He wore a white hat. He'd told us before that if he caught any of us picking on someone that he'd put a stop to it. I believed him, too.

But then, after hearing his country accent and re-examining his old-fashioned getup, I panicked. I saw, in that moment, the people who were bullying me. I left his room.

I still wonder what would have happened if I had spoken up.

I was failing two subjects. I didn't care about grades or attendance anymore. I was either in survival mode or thinking of ways I could die.

Every morning on the way to school, I felt like throwing up. There was a perpetual knot in my stomach. Every little sound made me jump. Voices coming down the hall elicited such a panic in me that I felt like running away.

I started spending lunch on the stage in the empty auditorium. I had to sneak away from everyone else to get there. The floor was always dirty and it was dark, but it felt safe.

I'd take bathroom breaks during class to get away from everyone. Sometimes I'd bang my head into the metal part of the toilets, hoping that I'd knock myself out and be sent to a hospital. I beat myself with my fists at home. I cried into my pillow. I thought of the gun underneath my parents' bed.

I remember pressing the gun to the side of my head and being surprised at how heavy it felt in my hand, like the iron core of a little planet.

Shooting myself wasn't turning out to be as easy as I'd imagined it to be. My hand was shaking. Was the gun even loaded? Would it fire if I pulled the trigger? I wasn't sure. My resolve began to weaken. I thought of my parents. I thought of my sister.

Growing up in the Oklahoma countryside, of course my family had guns. But I'd never handled one except for the time my dad had taken me out to the creek behind the house and had me shoot a log in the water. Back then, even while he was watching me, it had felt like I had a rattler by the tail. I was so afraid of it reaching back and biting me somehow.

Tears were rolling down my cheeks. I knew if I put the gun down then, I wouldn't do it at all.

"Boys will be boys," Principal Hoffman told my mother on the phone when she called. She was concerned for me.

If there was one person in the faculty who I believed actually, really hated me, it was Principal Hoffman. She knew exactly what was going on, but never did a thing to stop it.

My parents would have stopped it if they knew the extent of what was happening. But I couldn't tell them. I was too ashamed. I didn't know how to tell them without admitting I was gay, and in Cache, being gay was the worst thing you could be.

Boys will be boys.

I used to go to football games with my classmates. I sat with them on the concrete bleachers on cold November nights. I'd gone to the buffalo auctions where we ate burgers and listened to the auctioneer rattle off numbers. I'd decorated the pickup trucks with red and white streamers for the homecoming parade with them and ridden in the truck bed with my feet hanging off the back.

I did whatever they did without thinking too much about it. We were all Oklahoma kids. I was just part of the way of life there.

There were times I wondered, *when did I suddenly become different and when exactly did they learn to hate me?*

I never got a satisfying answer. Just "boys will be boys."

I hugged my mother tightly, sniffling into her blouse.

She said she had taken a teaching job at a high school in Lawton and that, even though I didn't live in the district, I could go to school there.

She promised me I wouldn't have to go back to Cache. I used to think Cache was the whole world. I'd traveled outside of it before, but still. When you're young, you think wherever you live is everything.

.

BANDIT IN BOLEY

Pretty Boy Floyd's chief lieutenant met his match in an all-black
Oklahoma town.

By *Jamie Birdwell-Branson*

THE AIR WAS COLD AND BITTER the day George Birdwell robbed
the Farmers and Merchants Bank in Boley, Oklahoma. Normally bus-
tling, the town was quiet the morning of November 23, 1932, the day
before Thanksgiving. Birdwell and his accomplices, Charles Glass and
C.C. Patterson, ate breakfast at a farmer's house before heading toward
Boley on Highway 62 in their roadster. The men were silent as they
drove into town.

Birdwell was the accomplice and "chief lieutenant" to Charles "Pretty Boy" Floyd, the infamous outlaw who wreaked havoc on American
banks in the early 20th century. That morning, though, Floyd was not
with his trusty sidekick.

After pulling off a string of robberies in Earlsboro, Maud, Mill Creek,
Roff, and Henryetta, Birdwell set his sights on robbing the Farmers and
Merchants Bank in Boley, despite Floyd's warnings against it. Friends
had warned Floyd of the dangers of robbing a bank in Boley. Floyd knew
that Birdwell, who was part Irish and six feet tall, would stand out in the
all-black town and that it could be too risky. Birdwell ignored his advice.

The criminal sauntered into the bank, taking the five or six steps to
the white marble counter. Pointing his gun, he barked orders at bank
president D.J. Turner to hand over the money in the till.

When Turner retrieved the last dollar, an alarm sounded. Birdwell was furious. He asked Turner if he pulled the alarm. Defiant, Turner said he had; Birdwell shot him in the chest with his .45 pistol.

George Birdwell murdered a prominent citizen in Boley, and, in an instant, changed the history of Boley forever. I know this story, not because I read it in a book, but because George Birdwell was my great-great-grandfather.

————————

Birdwell grew up in Oklahoma and was Irish, Cherokee, and Choctaw. He married a woman named Flora, who was always referred to as "Bob" by friends and family, and they had four children together. Birdwell worked in the oil field and moved to Earlsboro, Oklahoma, with his family when he got a job with Magnolia Oil.

Birdwell befriended his neighbor, Bradley Floyd, who later introduced him to his brother Charles Floyd. In early 1930, Birdwell was laid off at his job at Magnolia and desperately needed a way to feed his wife, four children, and two nephews who lived with the family. He began bootlegging whiskey and had some poker winnings, but it wasn't enough. He started robbing banks with Pretty Boy and soon became known as a Robin Hood figure, frequently doling out $20 to friends and neighbors in need.

"I don't really think that he would have turned out like that if the times hadn't been what they were," Birdwell's grandson, Robert Birdwell Sr.—my grandfather—told me. "When you've got a family to feed, there isn't money or jobs—that's just what he felt like he could turn to."

Birdwell's life reads like a John Wayne script. A story in *The Daily Oklahoman* on October 17, 1931, details an account of Birdwell kidnapping a deputy sheriff in Earlsboro and detaining him so that Birdwell could go to a funeral home to view his father, who had recently died. If Birdwell had attended his father's funeral, he would have been arrested for robbing banks in Earlsboro, Maud, Mill Creek, and Roff, Oklahoma. After Birdwell saw his father's body, he returned the deputy sheriff's gun on the outskirts of town, and rode into the sunset with Pretty Boy Floyd.

But Birdwell and Floyd's days were numbered. Their names and faces were routinely in the papers, and the FBI was just waiting for one of them to make a mistake. Boley was Birdwell's biggest mistake.

"Pretty Boy told the gang, 'Go anywhere else, but do not rob Boley. The people there need their money and they do not have much of it in the bank,' " said Henrietta Hicks, Boley municipal judge and unofficial historian. "They just would not listen. You know how Napoleon met his Waterloo? Well, George Birdwell met his Boley-loo."

Boley was one of about 50 all-black towns in Oklahoma settled by former slaves of Native Americans. After the Civil War, the U.S. government forced tribes in Indian Territory to free their slaves and give them all the rights of a tribal citizen, which included land ownership. From this land ownership, black "freedmen" settled together and became business owners, creating a haven in the South that acted as a shelter from the harsh reality of Jim Crow.

Boley was incorporated in 1905 and built on land that was given to Abigail Barnett, the daughter of a Creek freedman. Boley boasted a thriving economy and even dazzled the famous Booker T. Washington, who called the town "the most enterprising, and in many ways the most interesting, of the Negro towns in the U.S."

The town eventually grew large enough that it needed its own banks, one of which was the Farmers and Merchants Bank, managed by David Johnson Turner (or D.J., as he was known). Turner was an influential businessman who owned a pharmacy in Boley and was instrumental in starting one of the only black-owned banks in the country at the time. Birdwell didn't know this, and didn't anticipate the preparation of Boley's citizens against the attack.

"They [Birdwell and his gang] came in on the first day of bird-hunting season," Hicks said. The townspeople were armed with rifles, shovels, picks, and hoes.

"They had known Pretty Boyd Floyd was robbing these banks, so they were on alert," Hicks said. "They had rigged an alarm system in the bank, and when the last dollar was pulled out, the alarm would go off."

Birdwell didn't get the opportunity to make a clean getaway. Just moments after he killed Turner, bank bookkeeper H.C. McCormick took a shot at Birdwell from the safety of the bank vault. It was a clear and fatal one.

Birdwell's ragtag team of bandits didn't fare well, either. C. C. Patterson, who had run to his leader's aid after he heard the commotion, was greeted by the townspeople, who were armed with guns intended for the birds. Charles Glass, driver of the getaway car, tried to speed out of town but was quickly caught by the gunfire of Langston McCormick, the town sheriff. He survived and was driven to the hospital.

Hicks said that Langston McCormick chose not to kill Patterson because he didn't want to incite a race riot.

"We were not looking for a militia," she said. "The town was looking to protect their assets. The assets they had belonged to only black folk, whereas black folk at one time could not even put their money in some banks. We had our own bank, and that's what they were trying to protect."

If you visit Boley today, you can see a glimmer of the gem that this town must have once been. The wilting brick buildings and the bullet holes in the broken windows lend to a deep sense of sadness for a decaying town.

Sadness turns into hopefulness, however, when powerful group of Boley ladies—Municipal Judge Henrietta Hicks, Mayor Joan Matthews, and Chamber of Commerce President Fran Shelton—huddle together to figure out who to call to patch up the broken window.

"Boley is still alive and will stay alive based on those who continue to know its history," Shelton said.

Although George Birdwell's robbery was traumatic for the town, it wasn't crippling. Hicks said they tell the story of the Boley robbery, not because the story is great, but because it shows the strength and tenacity of African American people.

"There's no way [the robbery] could have been debilitating," Hicks said. "They had come from slavery. The people in Boley were a loving group and were so glad to be away from the oppressive regime of Southern white folk."

The robbery at the Farmers and Merchants Bank may not have been debilitating for the town of Boley, but was life-changing for Birdwell's young family. Wade Birdwell, my great-grandfather, George's son, lost his father when he was just 13 years old and was forced to support his three younger siblings and mother while completing his education.

"I think my dad always had an inferiority complex because of what his dad did," my grandfather told me. "I know it bothered him a lot. It put a big hardship on my dad because he was the sole supporter of the family. I always admired my dad for that."

The Birdwell family moved to California after George's death, and his wife eventually remarried. My great-grandfather Wade moved back to Oklahoma shortly after his first son was born. I believe he struggled over whether or not his father was a good man. Though he suffered the traumatic loss of his father, Wade was able to raise a family and lead a somewhat normal life.

Wade obliged a few of the historians who dropped by his house to interview him, but he rarely spoke of his infamous father to his family. He granted Michael Wallis a rare interview for his book *Pretty Boy: The Life and Times of Charles Arthur Floyd*. Wade was still willing to defend his father's name, even after his classmates had teased him mercilessly in school for being the son of a bank robber, and after he was forced to support his entire family off a grocery store clerk and paper route salary when his father died. He never spoke a bad word about his father, even though his family was looked down upon by those who knew the story. He wanted so badly to believe his father was a good man and shared some of his father's advice to Michael Wallis, saying: "He said way back then that there were two kinds of people who robbed—some who did it with a gun and some with an ink pen."

I just wish he hadn't chosen the gun.

NEAR MCALESTER

It's a place defined by munitions and metal bars, but it means much more than that to the people who live there.

By *Rilla Askew*

WHEN FOLKS ASK ME where in Oklahoma I live, I say "near McAlester," because this is where I go to shop, use the library, eat out, get my oil changed. It has the post office I visit most often, the courthouse I've been inside more than any other. I've set portions of two novels and a short story here. The town is seated deep in my consciousness, its history wedded to my own in ways that are difficult to tease out. The stories blend—fiction I've written, history, current reality, my family's old connections.

My Papaw Allie died here—at McAlester Regional Hospital. In his prime he worked here, at the munitions depot southwest of town. His first cousin Hughie Askew worked as a guard at the prison in the 1930s and was kidnapped by two inmates, shot in the neck, driven in the prison mail truck six miles west of the penitentiary, and let go when the escapees commandeered another car. Cousin Hughie survived. I don't know what happened to the prisoners. My daddy first worked here when he was 16, just as World War II was starting. He and Papaw would rise in the pre-dawn hours and drive 50 miles from Red Oak to work at the munitions plant.

These days, at 11:30 most mornings, my rock house a dozen miles east of McAlester will shake suddenly with the sound of distant booms.

The windows rattle. Framed photographs slip sideways on the walls. The trembling is like an earthquake, except for the ordered rhythm of the low, thunderous *boom*s that precede the vibrations. When my husband and I first heard them, we thought drilling companies were exploding dynamite deep in the earth, fracking for natural gas. It turns out fracking doesn't make that kind of a noise. The booms are, in fact, explosions: old ordnance being destroyed at the same munitions plant where my father and grandfather worked 70 years ago.

Around the time of statehood, I'm told, McAlester's civic leaders had a choice—would they rather have a land grant college located here or the state penitentiary? They chose the prison because they believed it meant more jobs. Today the prison is one of the area's main employers, along with the munitions plant, which was brought here through political pull and the promise of good available labor—out-of-work coal miners with strong backs, excellent work habits, and hungry families to feed. McAlester has long had a politically powerful history. It was the stomping grounds of Speaker of the House Carl Albert, who, in 1963, was a heartbeat away from the presidency, and the birthplace of former governor, lieutenant governor, and favored namesake to countless public buildings and thoroughfares all over Oklahoma, George Nigh. It was also the home of the longest serving state senator in U.S. history, Gene Stipe.

I like the looks of the town, and the character of its people, a smooth amalgam of Southern and Western—that signature Oklahoma blend that shows up in their accents, their attitude, their friendliness and style. They're good people, honest, hard working. In fact, the strong work ethic here is one of the area's calling cards. At a ceremony at the McAlester Army Ammunition Plant recently, the departing commander praised the civilian workers, how effective they are at loading and filling warheads, their speed at shipping large amounts of munitions quickly, their efficiency and safety record. When I take my car to my mechanic here, I know the work will be good, the price fair, the assessment honest.

I like the beautiful old Scottish Rite Consistory rising majestic on the town's highest hill: You can see it for miles at night, glowing a lovely amber-rose color. I like the Western style of the buildings, the rectangular eminence of the old Aldridge Hotel. I like how close to *now* the town's history remains. McAlester is one of the oldest towns in the state, founded, like so many Indian Territory towns, by an entrepreneurial white man who married an Indian woman. The first opera house west of the Mississippi was located here, but it was torn down to make way for the First Baptist Church parking lot.

Still, much of the original Old West feel remains. You can see it in Old Town on North Main Street, where J.J. McAlester's store still stands with its roofed porch and painted brick sides. The store and its owner make their literary appearance in Charles Portis' novel *True Grit*. McAlester, in fact, has multiple literary connections.

John Berryman, one of America's most influential poets, was born here, spent his childhood here. I like to ponder how the Pulitzer Prize-winning author of *Dream Songs* was shaped by this town. He left at the age of 10, never to return, but maybe McAlester's memory lingered in his sudden moves through rhetorical styles—the elevated language cutting quickly to plain diction, an uncouth tone. Or with Father Boniface, the adored priest under whom he served Mass here six days a week, who appears in Berryman's fiction, his conversation, his poems.

The great African American novelist Ralph Ellison never forgot a journey he took to McAlester as a boy—in a Jim Crow railcar with his mother and younger brother because she'd been promised a job of work in the town. The job never materialized and they returned to Oklahoma City, but that ride never left him; it's enshrined in his story "Boy on a Train," where the mother says: "Things are hard for us colored folks, son, and we have to stick together. Things is hard and we have to fight... O Lord, we have to fight!"

In March of 1935, local coal miners and their wives took over the county courthouse here for three days, demanding aid from the government: food and jobs and clothes. I based the climactic scene of my novel *Harpsong* on that siege, which happened, in reality, in the very courthouse where, in 2004, Terry Nichols was tried on state charges for his role in the bombing of Oklahoma City. I sat in on those proceedings. Nichols wasn't sentenced to death, as the state's law-and-order predilections would suggest, but to life in prison—which he was already serving at the federal facility at Leavenworth, Kansas, where he was returned to finish out his sentence. I suppose if he's ever paroled, Oklahoma will get him back and send him to die of old age at Big Mac.

If you come to McAlester by way of the Indian Nations Turnpike, you'll pass a statue of a cowboy in prison stripes arched high in the air on the back of a bucking bronco in honor of the annual prison rodeo, for decades the town's biggest tourist draw, although the prison rodeo hasn't been held since 2009—due to cost, is the official word, though I suspect there may be more to it than that. If you look north you'll see the penitentiary itself, a white shimmer on the horizon as you drive into town on a boulevard named for that U.S. congressman who was a heartbeat away from the presidency. You'll pass the red-brick courthouse with its u-shaped wings where Terry Nichols was tried, plus a ubiquity of buffaloes: handsome bronzed statues on most every corner honoring the local high school team mascot. If you keep going, you'll bisect George Nigh Expressway.

Don't trouble yourself to look for Gene Stipe Boulevard though. That street's name was changed back to Electric Avenue after the senator's political demise. Stipe was known to friend and foe alike as the Prince of Darkness, and he was powerful in this state almost beyond reckoning—until he wasn't any more. He was related to my family by marriage and helped us out in troubling times. Senator Stipe always showed up for funerals and pie suppers, that important Southeastern Oklahoma custom where local Masons auction off pies for thousands of dollars to help families in need due to medical bills and lack of health insurance. I have good memories of the Prince of Darkness. He was a marvelous storyteller and could be extremely charming. A power broker he may have been, but he always showed up for his people. He showed up for my family.

Every few months a quiet vigil takes place in McAlester, outside the prison walls, as another man or woman is executed. The anti-death penalty activists, the Quakers and Christians and committed believers all stand about with their homemade signs and their silence. We only hear about such things when the execution is botched, as it was in the 45-minute torturous death of Clayton Lockett. Otherwise the vigils do not draw much attention.

The prison rodeo drew plenty of attention in its day. Crowds came from all over the country. I remember going as a child and wondering at how the guards and the prisoners seemed to get along so well. I had thought they would be enemies, like the enemies we drop our bombs on, but they acted like friends. There, inside the prison walls, in the billowing dust beneath the tall prison lights, midst the shouts and smells and the announcer's loud metallic voice and the great thundering excitement, they did anyway.

Today, all of the conventional bombs our country drops on other countries are made in McAlester, at the same plant where the old bombs and ammunition that haven't been used to destroy enemies are themselves destroyed, to make way for fresh new ones.

In some ways the prison and the munitions plant represent McAlester to me, as McAlester represents Oklahoma, as Oklahoma represents the rest of the nation—each an exquisite distillation of the American character. I love this place, though sometimes not its politics. I love how the past remains alive here, though sometimes I hate our true history. I love the people and the landscapes and the buildings and this state and this little town itself, though sometimes they break my heart.

I used to believe that my dad and granddad made bombs and ammunition to kill enemies during World War II. When I asked Daddy about it, though, he said, no, they worked in construction: They didn't build bombs but built the buildings where the bombs would be built. My friends and neighbors who work at the munitions plant today probably don't see an Iraqi boy with his arms blown off by one of our bombs, or the slaughtered Afghan wedding party, bride and groom and guests in shreds and bloody pieces, from a U.S. drone strike's mistake.

I don't expect them to. These are good people working good jobs, the best jobs to be had in the area, with decent salaries, benefits, child care—things people need to take care of their families. I see them, though. The armless boy. The slaughtered bride. Most mornings around 11:30, when I hear the powerful, muted *boom* in the distance, and my house begins to quake.

Just as, when local news tells me it's time, I see, in my mind's eye, a living, breathing man led in manacles along a blank cinder block hall into a small room with curtained windows and clinical looking IV lines and, there in the center beneath bright florescent lights, a clean, white-sheeted gurney, surrounded by good people working good jobs.

THREE

PROFILES FROM THE MIDDLE

AMONG THE TRIBE
OF THE WANNABES

How Iron Eyes Cody made a career out of pretending to be an
Indian, and why white people continue to fashion Native
identities out of thin air.

By *Russell Cobb*

LET'S TAKE A VOYAGE to a not-so-distant land and visit a strange
tribe. Or maybe not so strange. In fact, you may even belong to it. Before
we begin our expedition, a trivia question: What do Bill Clinton, Miley
Cyrus, Johnny Cash, and Elizabeth Warren all have in common?

Answer: All of them have claimed to be part Cherokee, but none
have been able to prove it. Not that any of these celebrities are unique in
this regard. Rare is the Oklahoma family that doesn't think it possesses
at least one-sixteenth Cherokee blood.

But here's a fun fact: according to the Cherokee Nation, there are
approximately 120,000 tribal members living in the state, which has a
population of 3.8 million people. That's only about 3 percent of Oklahomans. The tribe we're going to visit, however, is bigger than the Cherokee Nation and perhaps even bigger than the entire state of Oklahoma—although that's difficult confirm, since the Census Bureau doesn't
keep statistics on this subset of the population.

We are among the tribe of the Wannabes: non-Native Americans
who insist on claiming Indian heritage. Why do Wannabes appropriate,
fabricate, and invent a Native identity? Is it for pure financial gain? Is it
part of a colonialist project to speak for the Other? College admissions?
A highly subjective existential crisis? Examining the motives of the

Wannabes is a fraught subject, one where good intentions rub up against old racist habits and where narrative embroidery easily morphs into self-delusion. It's where the personal is political and politics get personal.

Our voyage begins in earnest with the case of Iron Eyes Cody, a man better known to the world as "The Crying Indian."

If you watched TV at any time in the 1970s, you'll remember the Crying Indian. He debuted on television on Earth Day, 1971, in an event some people have called the birth of the modern environmental movement. The ad, produced by the pro-bono advertising group the Ad Council, is one of the most emotionally powerful one-minute spots ever produced.

It begins with a vague image of a man in a canoe barely visible through the leaves of a tree. He paddles gently down a river to a slow thud of drums. The fringe from his buckskin jacket, two braids of long hair, and a single feather in his headband come into view. We briefly glimpse the idyllic image of unspoiled America: pine trees, a glistening lake, and a Noble Savage in a canoe. Here is the natural man as Jean-Jacques Rousseau once imagined him: the human being at one with nature and freed from the shackles of societal conventions.

Now we are face-to-face with our stoic warrior. He paddles with more vigor as the tempo of the music picks up. The camera zooms in on two pieces of garbage in the water. A brassy soundtrack starts to blare, and the camera sweeps out to reveal a factory belching smoke into the air and more litter in the lake. Our Noble Savage drags his canoe to a shoreline littered with plastic cups and aluminum cans, his head bowed in sorrow.

He walks to a road filled with traffic, his once-stoic face now show-ing signs of a profound sadness as he watches garbage being tossed out of passing cars.

An off-screen baritone narrator intones the following: "Some peo-ple have a deep, abiding respect for the natural beauty that was once this country. And some people don't." A plastic sack dropped by a motorist explodes at our Wise Elder's feet, his buckskin now soiled by fast food.

The narrator pauses a beat, allowing a sense of collective shame to wash over the audience. The narrator starts back in again. "People start pollution, and people can stop it." A single tear wells up and then rolls down the Indian's cheek as the screen fades to black.

Many people have wondered about this tragic figure, and in his 1982 memoir, *Iron Eyes: My Life as a Hollywood Indian*, Cody purported to give a full account of his life. He tells us he was born and raised on a ranch in Oklahoma to family of Cree and Cherokee farmers, only finding fame years later as a character actor and consultant on Indian dress and sign language to famous directors such as Cecil B. DeMille and John Ford.

Iron Eyes traced his ancestry all the way back to the Trail of Tears. During the Civil War, his Cherokee grandfather joined up with a bunch of Confederate outlaws known as Quantrill's Raiders. This mixed-race posse terrorized Missouri, Kansas, and Indian Territory, pillaging Union forces and riding off into the Ozarks with their loot. They were indomitable, submitting neither to the Confederate military brass nor to the victorious Union army. They were, in effect, professional badasses— some wearing black sombreros with silver inlays and bullet bandoliers across their chests. Among their posse was a black man named Two Bits who acquired the name for his piano-playing in whorehouses. If this is starting to sound like a Sam Peckinpah or Quentin Tarantino Western, remember that Iron Eyes' memoir is subtitled: *My Life as a Hollywood Indian*.

But Iron Eyes, well, according to his memoir, was just a regular old "Injun" who "wandered off the reservation into fame and fortune." The fact there were no Indian reservations in Oklahoma and that the eastern portion of the state—which included the Cherokee area—was known not as Oklahoma Territory (as Iron Eyes calls it) but Indian Territory, and that statehood occurred when he was just two years old, might raise a red flag among literal-minded readers. But for the sake of our journey, let's give him a pass. We'll assume he is speaking meta-phorically of "the reservation." In any case, the narrative quickly shifts from an undisclosed location on an Oklahoma ranch to Hollywood, as Iron Eyes recounts a lifetime of work during the Golden Age of the Hollywood Western, and it is here we see the formation of the iconic American Indian take shape.

Most of the first half of the book is devoted to celebrity yarn spin-
ning, recalling Gary Cooper's terrible horsemanship and incorrigible
playboy vices. Or John Wayne's terrible alcoholism and fear that his real
name—Marion Morrison—sounded like a "fairy." More importantly,
however, the book reveals the solidification of the American imaginary
regarding Native Americans. Iron Eyes recalls how he butted heads with
the legendary Cecil B. DeMille, insisting that Indians be represented
"authentically" in the filming of *The Plainsman*. On set, Cody assembled
a cast of "Indians," some belonging to local tribes but mostly white
actors dressed in headdresses and war paint:

> Everybody stood at attention while he walked up and down
> the ranks. "Okay, take that off," he said, stopping at one
> end, pointing to a beaded vest. He stopped again, "Take
> that off, and that, and—" "Wait, wait a minute, C.B. You
> can't take those things off. He's gonna be a chief. Cheyenne
> chiefs wore vests like that. And he's a warrior, they always
> wore leggings. That's a medicine pouch on him. It stays."
> "You've got too much clothes on them." "Not for these
> Indians, C.B. We either do an authentic picture or I'll walk
> off and the Indians will come with us." [1]

Iron Eyes also taught actors a few rudimentary Plains Indian
sign-language gestures. Cherokees are not Plains Indians, but somehow
Iron Eyes established himself as an authority on the subject. Some tribes
have different gestures, but Iron Eyes created a fusion, an Esperanto of
hand talk. In 1970, he documented this language in a book called *Indian
Talk: Hand Signals of the American Indians*. The book was reviewed pos-
itively by one of the most prestigious scholarly journals in anthropology,
American Anthropologist, in 1972.

As Hollywood moved from the era of pure spectacle and illusion to
a politicized and realistic aesthetic in the late 1960s, Iron Eyes followed
suit. Working with the mercurial British actor Richard Harris on the
1970 *A Man Called Horse*, Cody began to insist on authentic portray-

---

1   Cody and Perry, 1982: 194–195.

als of initiation rites and medicine rituals, often over the demands of the producer.

Although Iron Eyes played bit parts in dozens of Westerns over five decades, it is this film that may hold the clue to his transformation from a supporting actor into America's most recognizable Indian. *A Man Called Horse* tells the story of an English aristocrat, John Morgan, who is captured by the Sioux and enslaved by them until his cunning and dogged determination wins the Natives over and he becomes a Sioux warrior. Unlike previous Westerns, however, *A Man Called Horse* spared the Armenian bole (a reddish-brown chemical often sprayed on white actors to make them look Native) and convinced many moviegoers that they were finally catching a glimpse of authentic Plains Indian culture.

Some Native American activists, however, saw the film as inauthentic. Among them was Ward Churchill, who wrote that the movie "depicts a people whose language is Lakota, whose hairstyles range from Assiniboine through Nez Perce to Comanche, whose tipi design is Crow, and whose Sun Dance ceremony and lodge in which it is held are both typically Mandan."

Churchill's critique hinged on a strident defense that "authenticity" is something that can only be defined from within a given culture. Churchill, like Iron Eyes Cody, claimed part Cherokee ancestry, and set about defining the parameters of Indian authenticity in books like *Fantasies of the Master Race*. Churchill himself, however, turned out to be more parts Wannabe than Cherokee.[2]

---

2   Churchill continually cautioned readers that Wannabes or "Friends of the Indian" — such as the Richard Harris character — are almost always neocolonialist wolves in sheep's clothing. The best white people could do, in his opinion, was to sit back and listen deeply to real Indians such as himself. In 2005, Churchill began to be hoisted on his own petard. Following academic misconduct allegations, the Cherokee Nation retreated from Churchill, saying that he only possessed "associate membership" as an honor, and that all associated memberships were rescinded in the 1990s. Like Elizabeth Warren, Churchill refused to back down, and presented evidence that may identify him as one-sixteenth Cherokee.

By the early 1970s, then, Iron Eyes Cody was not only simply a Native-American character actor, but one of the most important figures in fashioning Americans' ideas about the "authentic Indian." The culmination of his long career was undoubtedly the "The Crying Indian." The Ad Council, a pro-bono conglomeration of companies that creates public service announcements, sponsored the commercial. Rosie the Riveter, Smokey Bear, "Just Say No": all public service announcements produced by the Ad Council. During the Cold War, the Ad Council turned to blatant U.S. propaganda, urging Americans to take an active role in promoting U.S. industry in the fight against communism. At the same time, the modern environmental movement was born and urged industry to promote recycling and reuse of materials. The Ad Council countered with its own "environmental" message, which stressed the responsibility of individuals—not corporations—to fight pollution.

One of the taglines of this Keep America Beautiful campaign was "People start pollution. People can stop it," which seemed benign enough, but turned out to be part of a political attack on more progressive environmental groups such as the Sierra Club. Keep America Beautiful was a non-profit group supported by bottle manufacturers to prevent bottle deposit laws, and encouraging more and more consumption, according to investigative journalist Ginger Strand. Bottle deposit laws—most enacted with the birth of the environmental movement—were driving down demand for new glass and aluminum. The Ad Council's "Crying Indian" spots tried to change the conversation, making the environmental movement a question of personal ethics, not corporate responsibility.

Iron Eyes initially declined the role as the Crying Indian. He didn't know how to swim and was afraid to be out in a canoe in San Francisco Bay by himself. The director promised to have a helicopter hover over him in case he tipped over. When it came time for the money shot—the tear rolling down the cheek—Iron Eyes was ready. He knew how to cry on demand for the camera, but there was a problem: His real tears did not show up well enough on camera. The director used glycerin to created one large tear that rolled down Iron Eyes's cheek at the last minute.

In 1996, the journalist Angela Aleiss revealed that the man known to the world as "The Crying Indian" was born Espera Oscar de Corti in the small town of Kaplan, Louisana. Aleiss told me it was an open secret among Native American actors in Los Angeles that Iron Eyes wasn't Indian, but no one had thought to figure out who he really was.

Aleiss consulted records from a small Catholic church in the town and found that de Corti's father, Antonio, had been the victim of vicious anti-Italian sentiment in turn-of-the-century Louisiana. The decade before Oscar's father came over from Sicily, more than a dozen Italians in the state had been lynched. To make matters worse, an extortion racket commonly referred to as the Black Hand Society (an early version of the Mafia) had sprung up in southern Louisiana. Antonio de Corti had to give up his small shop and flee to Texas, where his three sons eventually joined him.

Somewhere along the way, young Oscar de Corti saw a Wild West show and became enamored with all things Native, always playing the Indian in Cowboys and Indians. Aleiss wrote that the de Corti family remade themselves in Texas; the father slightly Anglicized his name to Tony Corti. Oscar made his way to Los Angeles in the teens, becoming Oscar Codey and finally Iron Eyes Cody. By the time Aleiss interviewed him in 1996, he had been widowed by his Native wife and brought up the two sons they adopted from a Navajo reservation. When he died in 1999, everything indicated that he convinced himself of his own lie.

———————

Iron Eyes Cody may have been a Hollywood Indian, but there's more to the tribe than show business. There are many subcategories of Wannabes, but the most common member of the tribe we might call the Almost Native—the white person who claims one-sixteenth blood quantum, just enough to squeak by America's arbitrary racial standards that designate who is and is not a minority.

The most famous and most controversial Almost Native of the moment is Oklahoma City-born Elizabeth Warren, who is rumored to be a candidate for president in 2016. During her 2012 campaign for the U.S. Senate in Massachusetts against incumbent Senator Scott Brown, Warren frequently described "family lore" about her Cherokee forbearers as part of her hardscrabble coming-of-age story. Conservatives mocked her for identifying herself as a "Native American" minority during two stints at law schools in the 1990s. While it appears that she never benefited from affirmative action for minorities and stopped listing herself as a minority lawyer by 1995, she has refused to back away from claims of Native ancestry.

When Warren's claims to Cherokee ancestry were scrutinized closely by genealogists, no one could find her ancestors among those named on the Dawes Roll, which the government intended to be a master list of Cherokee surnames and finalized in 1906. (Although they did find one ancestor during territorial days who had actually boasted of killing a Cherokee.) Like many dubious narratives of whites passing for Native, Warren's story takes many twists and turns, some of which receive a gloss in her new memoir, *A Fighting Chance.* In the book, Warren weaves her "Native-American heritage" (specific references to the Cherokee have now disappeared) into a narrative of working-class struggle, with her "mamaw and papaw" handing down stories and recipes from their days in Indian Territory.

And then there's Aunt Bee, who told Liz Warren that her papaw had inherited high cheekbones from his Indian ancestors but did not pass them down to the little girl. It's all part of a home-spun narrative of authentic Americana: Daddy worked hard as a janitor, but had a heart attack and couldn't pay the medical bills. Mama was devoted to her family, but sometimes didn't have enough money to put food on the table for the four kids. Eventually, little Liz had to work, too, before she dropped out of college at age 19 to support her husband's professional goals. Then she picked herself up by her bootstraps and put herself through law school in the wake of a divorce. It's like a PG-rated Loretta Lynn or Tammy Wynette song with all the cheating and drinking purged from the storyline.

A lot of people scoffed at fair-skinned, blue-eyed Warren's claim of Native-American heritage. But, as an Okie myself, I instantly recognized the narrative. It has an undeniable pull and a certain degree of truthiness, as Stephen Colbert would say. The mythic Native ancestor in the white settler family lends a folksy, feel-good element to a narrative of colonization, exploitation, and plunder.

We still are left with a nagging question for the Wannabes: Why do they do it? Why do so many white people—from Elizabeth Warren to Miley Cyrus to Iron Eyes Cody—fashion a Native identity out of thin air? I contacted Aleiss about her research to ask her if there was anything that united this unruly tribe. The one common denominator she cited was "financial opportunity." Indeed, there are many instances of whites making a buck while trafficking in faux-Native identity, but I'm not totally convinced it all boils down to money. According to the 2010 census, more than a quarter of Native Americans live in poverty, contrasted to only 10 percent of whites. There's more money to be made in the white world than on the reservation.

I suspect that the claim of Native identity bestows upon a prospective author a sort of symbolic capital that works in inverse proportion to white privilege. Fake Indian personae have allowed otherwise un-publishable white authors to achieve notoriety. There are many examples, including Forrest Carter, the author of *The Education of Little Tree*. Carter turned out to not be Cherokee, as he claimed, but a former Ku Klux Klansman from Alabama named Asa Earl Carter. The case of Carter's memoir is laden with even more ironic twists and turns than that of Iron Eyes Cody, as Carter made a name for himself in the public sphere by becoming one of Alabama's most vocal white supremacists. He is reputed to have written Alabama Governor George Wallace's *cri de guerre*: "Segregation now, segregation tomorrow, and segregation forever." Carter disappeared from public life only to remake himself years later as Forrest "Little Tree" Carter, an orphaned boy raised by his Cherokee grandparents, wise elders who taught the boy to live a simple, natural life until he confronts the racist system of an Indian residential school.

To this day, critics are divided about how to view *Little Tree*: Is the book an opportunistic play on white America's hunger for the "authentic" Indian, or is it Carter's secret confession of guilt for having been such a vocal racist for decades. The writer Sherman Alexie has summoned up this contradiction nicely: "*Little Tree* is a lovely little book, and I sometimes wonder if it is an act of romantic atonement by a guilt-ridden white supremacist, but ultimately I think it is the racial hypocrisy of a white supremacist."

Perhaps racial hypocrisy explains the extreme case of Asa Earl Carter, but there's undoubtedly something strange in the American psyche regarding the Wannabes, and I haven't been immune from their truth-y allure.

I owe my rather unusual middle name—St. Clair—to a notable Choctaw artist named St. Clair Homer, a man I once understood to be my maternal grandfather. As a boy, I hated my middle name. Who would name their boy St. Clair?

"Isn't that a girl's name?" I asked my mom one day.

My mom told me I should be proud of the name because St. Clair Homer was a famous artist and somehow (I wasn't quite sure how) a part of our family. Homer is known to the art world as Homma (the Choctaw work *homa* which means "red"—as in "Oklahoma").

Let's get this straight: Homma was no Wannabe. He traced a lineage back to Pushmataha, a general who fought the British in the War of 1812; his grandfather had been Secretary of the Choctaw Nation. The thing was, I wasn't quite sure if Homma was actually my grandfather because my grandmother started living with another man who wasn't Native at all. When I was three years old, though, Homma won first place in the Oklahoma Bicentennial Indian Art Exhibition at Gilcrease Museum for a bronze sculpture called "Spirit Horse." I was too young to remember the exhibit, but I saw it later during school field trips.

What struck me about Homma's work was its stark defiance of much of the art in Gilcrease. He engaged in a playful mocking of Western mythology. There was none of the rugged individualism of the American West: the white cowboy facing down the harsh environment and the Indian savages. In 1976, for the centennial of the Battle of Little Big Horn, Homma declared that he was going on "full war-path mode" and made a series satirical postcards "commemorating" the event.

In the meantime, I had learned the truth of my connection to Homma. My biological grandfather had died shortly after my mother was born during World War II. Homma and my grandmother lived together off and on for decades, and he practically raised my mom. Later, they drifted apart and my grandmother remarried.

His presence in my life was still there, however, especially every time anyone asked me about my middle name. My first year of college, I met a group of exchange students from Great Britain. I told them I was from Oklahoma, a place they only knew from the musical and Westerns.

"You must be part Indian or something," one of the Brits said. I thought about this for a minute. Yes, I must be part Indian. Not only am I named after one, I'm darker than most white people. The British exchange students really seemed interested. They clearly wanted to know an Indian.

"I think I'm part Choctaw," I said. "But only, like, one-sixteenth, so I'm not on any tribal roles or anything."

There, I'd done it. I felt good to be part Indian, as if I belonged to something big. Something noble, wise, and timeless. Now that I'd said it, it had to be true. After all, my mother's family came from rural eastern Oklahoma, right on the dividing line between the Choctaw and Cherokee Nations. The family's cemetery plot in Checotah was right next to the Indian section. And, like Liz Warren's Papaw, we had high cheekbones.

So I would belong to the tribe of the Wannabes for a while, especially during my early 20s, when I actually didn't know what the hell I was. The tribe gave me a sense of identity and it carried some instant prestige when traveling abroad. Europeans love Indians, I discovered. I never fully bought in, however. I knew plenty of people who tried to cash-in on some supposed Indian great-grandfather to qualify for a tuition break or minority status. That wasn't me.

There was one small problem: The only Indians I knew in Tulsa were a lot like me. They grew up on the same '80s pop music and TV shows, followed the same sports teams (even the Oklahoma Sooners, who got their name illegally stealing Native land in the late 19th century). They didn't ride horses and they didn't even have cool names, like Iron Eyes. Most of them weren't any darker than I was. So I didn't want to be them. I wanted to be like that Indian in that commercial, stoically paddling his canoe through the American landscape, offering a rebuke to the crass commercialism of mainstream America. Oh, wait…

FIRST CHARGED, LAST FREED

J.B. Stradford, a well-to-do black business man in Tulsa's prosperous Greenwood district, was the first charged with inciting the Tulsa Race Riot and the last to be exonerated.

By *Steve Gerkin*

JOHN THE BAPTIST MOVED TO TULSA IN 1899. The Stradford family called him J. B.[1] He was a former Kentucky slave who was not afraid to preach the gospel of equal treatment and racial solidarity for black Americans. College-educated in Ohio at Oberlin College, Stradford received his law degree from Indiana University, practicing in Indianapolis and yearning to influence black equality. Tulsa became his destiny. Leaders of the local white community yearned for his demise.

In America, the late 1800s provided an unpainted canvas of opportunity for post-emancipation blacks. They were free to relocate, joining up with other freshly freed blacks and freedmen from Creek enslavement to start communities separate from the white population. While

---

1 The slave master named his slaves, calling J. B.'s father Julius Caesar or J. C., but he had no legitimate last name until J.C. forged his master's name on a pass and escaped to Stratford, Ontario. Changing one letter, he adopted the surname of Stradford, earned enough money to return to Kentucky prior to Emancipation and secured legal documents declaring his family free. Many blacks used initials during that time period so that whites would not be able to disrespect them by using their first name.

racial distrust remained, their new beginnings were sites of burgeoning entrepreneurship.

Over 60 percent of the U.S. black population served whites as domestics, restaurant cooks, bootblacks, and laborers. Wages were brought back to their new settlements and spent with black grocers, black lumberyards, black saloons and gambling enterprises, black theaters, and a cadre of like-skinned businesses.

Oklahoma's future looked bright for blacks. Led by the vision of Edwin McCabe, founder of the first black community of Langston in 1890, the state became a mecca for black towns and self-reliant communities—50 by 1920.[2] The *New York Times* warned on March 1, 1890, that a Negro settlement is "a camp of savages." McCabe sent recruiters to the South, appealing to racial pride, and hoped to recruit enough blacks to become the majority race and force the whites to turn over the region to them.

McCabe's dream of a politically powerful, black-friendly state lured Stradford from Indianapolis to the dirt streets of Tulsa's undeveloped Greenwood area.

Buying up large tracts of undeveloped land northeast of the tracks that bordered downtown, 39-year-old J. B. Stradford sold his Greenwood parcels to blacks only. O.W. Gurley, the acknowledged founder of the new community, did the same as Black Tulsa took shape.

Yet, Stradford was not a real estate man by trade. He was a University of Indiana-educated attorney who used his investment profits to aggressively litigate for black social justice. Never shy to voice his outrage, he occasionally declared, "The day a member of our group was mobbed (lynched) in Tulsa, the streets would be bathed in blood." The activist put himself on the line to prevent lynches. In 1918 he turned back a lynching mob in Bristow, Oklahoma. When Stradford suffered Jim Crow discrimination, he did not sit idly.

Walking along Greenwood Avenue, a white deliveryman made a racist remark about Stradford. Nearly beating him to death, friends pulled Stradford off the bloodied iceman, telling him that if he killed

---

2 Census numbers show that the black population in 1890 of 250,000 ballooned to more than 2 million by 1920.

the white man, he would be mobbed, a euphemism for lynched. Later, he was acquitted for violating Oklahoma Jim Crow laws.

Riding a train from Kansas to Tulsa in 1912, nearly 50 years after the end of the Civil War, J. B. experienced the continuation of slave law in Oklahoma. When the locomotive reached the Oklahoma border, the conductor stopped the train and Stradford was forcibly removed from the black luxury car although he had paid the higher fare. Oklahoma exempted railroads from the expense of such cars if it did not make economic sense. Stradford sued Midland Valley Railroad in state and federal courts for false imprisonment. All courts ruled against his demand for justice by law, angering Greenwood residents.

In 1916, Stradford railed the Tulsa City Commission for its segregation ordinance that he claimed casts "a stigma upon the colored race in the eyes of the world; and to sap the spirit of hope for justice before the law from the race itself." The upside of segregation was the "white" dollars earned by black Tulsans stayed in the district, giving Deep Greenwood merchants the spoils of their neighbors, while the black print media continued to pull no punches.

The most militant black voice in America and a founder of the NAACP fanned the embers during a Greenwood speech. Brought to the community by Stradford and newspaperman A. J. Smitherman in March of 1921, the first black Harvard Ph.D., W. E. B. Du Bois, lectured the throngs that the hatred in the white man's heart was still strong. At times, the professor proposed that the only solution to hate is hate.

Du Bois argued in those times, "We have suffered and cowered... When the armed lynchers come, we too must gather armed. When the mob moves, we propose to meet it with sticks and clubs and guns." There was a rising tide of passion in Greenwood. They were ready to forcefully defend the promise of equality under the law.

White Tulsa became less enchanted with the likes of J.B. Stradford. Although Stradford was respected as a legitimate businessman, many Tulsans despised him.

Stradford and his close friend Andrew J. Smitherman, the owner/publisher of the black newspaper *Tulsa Star*, situated on Greenwood Avenue, spoke out against the trio of leading causes of civil rights in Oklahoma—lynching, voting rights, and the railroad segregation policy. *The Black Dispatch*, a black Oklahoma City newspaper published by

Roscoe Dunjee, regularly fired up Greenwood residents, declaring the courts were full of dead men's bones, denied enforcement of the United States Supreme Court decision guaranteeing black Oklahomans' right to vote, and validated Oklahoma's railroad segregation statute. During vaudeville shows at the famed Dreamland Theater on Greenwood, a frequently bantered slogan was "Don't let any white man run it over on you, but fight." Racial rhetoric primed Tulsa.

While inflammatory verbiage continued in district tabloids and on street corners, business was good. J. B. Stradford amassed a sizeable bank account. With 15 rental houses, including a 16-room brick apartment building, he earned a real estate income of nearly $8,000 a month in 2013 dollars.

Stradford decided it was time that black travelers of means should have accommodations as swank as downtown's Hotel Tulsa. He envisioned his hotel as the pinnacle of his dreams, remarking, "The Stradford would be a monument to the thrift, energy, and business tact of the race in Tulsa [and] to the race in the state of Oklahoma." The exuberant opening of his eponymous hotel on June 1, 1918, signified the realization of his promised land, adding credence to Booker T. Washington's description of this district as Black Wall Street.

The three-story edifice of pressed brick above the windows and stone slabs below cost a glitzy $50,000. The segregated Stradford, serving blacks only, was perhaps the largest black-owned and operated hotel in America. While it fulfilled his dream, the construction of the hotel created financial difficulties. Stradford ran out of money. Borrowing $20,000 helped, yet, when a boxcar of beds, rugs, and chandeliers rolled into the station, the new hotelier could not pay the $5,000 bill.

Within eyeshot of the hotel, the furnishings for the 54 modern "living rooms," gambling hall, dining hall, and saloon languished on the rails. Stradford negotiated paying a quarter of the total and the remainder in monthly payments. The Stradford Hotel at 301 N. Greenwood was open for business.

It was a gay time. A new form of music ricocheted up Greenwood Avenue from the dancehalls. Jazz, with its gyrating rhythms and freedom to improvise, stimulated the dancers and frightened the white community, who considered the music style as vibrations for the half-savage.

The piano in the Stradford Hotel pounded out jazz for its distinguished clientele who tripped the fantastic toe.

Amid the glamour of the Stradford, the racial tension in Greenwood and the region was superficially suppressed. Desperate events stoked emotions.

In April 1921, Greenwood celebrated the success of a group of Muskogee black men that stormed the city jail, liberated a black man (John McShane), and shot a white deputy sheriff in the process. The local black community justified the action, claiming they prevented a lynching. Their defiance energized Greenwood.

Stradford and Smitherman agreed that a community must be vigilant if a black man was in danger of being lynched. It was justice—a legal right, they reckoned, to take aggressive action, encouraging their community to support armed militancy towards lynching.

In the afternoon edition of May 30, 1921, the *Tulsa Tribune*, a front-page story announced a "negro will be lynched tonight." The following day, a Greenwood teenager, Dick Roland, was arrested under the allegations that he attempted to rape a 17-year-old white girl, Sarah Page, in an elevator. Although a grand jury indictment against him was rendered several days later and then dismissed within three months for lack of a prosecution witness (Sarah, according to oral histories from Greenwood survivors, was his taboo lover.), the yellow-journalism article fomented the deadliest and most destructive "riot" in the history of the United States—an event that would forever be referred to as the Tulsa Race Riot of 1921.

A. J. Smitherman's office of the *Tulsa Star* was the center of activity the night before the battle. Several carloads of passionate armed veterans made repeated trips from the newspaper's curb to the jail holding Roland, where they confronted a growing white mob. Dedicated to stop a lynching, J. B. held court with the gathering crowd, repeating his oft used statement about "blood in the streets." He recalled in his memoirs that he declared to the nervous onlookers what he would do if there were a lynching: "If I can't get anyone to go with me, I will go single-handed and empty my automatic into the mob and, then, resign myself to my fate." His comments encouraged men, including a tall, light-skinned veteran named O. B. Mann, to continue making trips to the courthouse.

Mann, a successful Greenwood grocer, returned from the war with inflated ideas about equality and sure he could take on the world, according to O. W. Gurley. He continued, during court testimony on an insurance claim relating to property damage from the riot, that it was the inadvertent discharge of Mann's handgun when grabbed by a white man that activated the fatal chain of events.

At dawn, the sound of an air horn commanded the heavily armed white armada, loaded with Klansmen, to step over the tracks and attack an underarmed band of black veterans in uniform and frightened Greenwood residents intent to defend their families and homes. Within a matter of hours, hundreds were murdered and homes and businesses were looted and burned as thousands of black Tulsans were arrested and herded into detention.

Dick Roland was a forgotten man. Sheriff McCollough claims Dick spent a safe evening in the county jail and was secreted out of town by 8 a.m. amidst the gunfire of the massacre, never, according to most, to return to Tulsa. The carnage would continue through the day.

The June 1, 1921, the evening edition of the *Tulsa Tribune* wrote that "a motley procession of negroes wended its way down Main Street to the baseball park with hands held high above their heads, their hats in one hand, a token of their submission to the white man's authority." The reporter continued, "They will return, not to their homes, but to heaps of ashes, the angry reprisal for the wrong inflicted on him by the inferior race." Some of that race-under-siege resisted the roundup.

Attempting to hold the mobsters from advancing, Stradford and others fired from the second-story porch that fronted the hotel. The building represented black equality to him and he preferred death rather than to lose it. The west-facing windows on the third-floor had been smashed by a machine gun. Six men were wounded and one was dead.

The hotel became a haven for black families. Most left, surrendering to the militia. A sobbing Augusta, Stradford's wife, pleaded with him, "Oh, Papa, let us go, too."

"If you want to go with the crowd, then go," he said. "I intend to protect my hotel."

Augusta stayed. Others returned with a message of hope. The militia had promised to keep the hotel from further destruction, if Stradford surrendered. He agreed.

A short, slightly rotund man with a pencil-thin mustache perched above his squared chin, the now 60-year-old Stradford was reportedly the wealthiest man in Greenwood with over $1.6 million dollars of investments in today's currency. He stood with his gun in the doorway of his hotel, waiting for the car of his captors. His dark, piercing eyes surveyed the burning buildings in Deep Greenwood. Hundreds of the 8,000 Greenwood residents ran through the street before him. Some with raised hands were marshaled to detention centers, shots fired at their feet and hopelessness on their faces.

A man described by descendants as having the strength of a Mandingo warrior, watched mobsters enter his building. They took him to the Convention Center where city officials took $2,000 of his money. There is no mention of Augusta's whereabouts. Stradford was not detained long, but he was still in harm's way.

One day later, an order asked for the arrest of Stradford so he could face a grand jury. The contention was he had encouraged carloads of armed blacks who organized and left from the Stradford Hotel. Without his presence, he was indicted for inciting a riot. The penalty for the charge was death or life imprisonment. The white community needed a definable villain and they decided on Stradford.

His name was well known in the Tulsa white community. His railroad segregation lawsuit as well as his defiance towards the segregation ordinance put him squarely in opposition to their values. He named a hotel after himself, so they knew he was a man of ambition. As Greenwood's Republican Party leader, the local papers named him a "henchman." Since the media labeled the riot a "Negro uprising," they reasoned that the wealthiest, most defiant and outspoken man must be the ringleader—and he fled, so he must be guilty.

With authorities on his heels, Stradford leaned back in a segregated railroad car headed for Independence, Kansas. Through a gentle rain, Stradford gazed up Greenwood Avenue spying his symbol of black pride, reduced to smoldering ashes and charred brick. Oklahoma was no longer the Promised Land.

Along with hundreds of black Americans who died on June 1, 1921, and thousands who had homes, businesses, and possessions stolen or burned, the Stradford Hotel laid in ruins, never to be reconstructed. The crown jewel of Black Tulsa shined a scant three years to the day.

On June 6, J. B. Stradford became the first person formally charged with inciting a riot. To be proven guilty, the county district attorney only needed to show he abetted the riot that resulted in murder, looting, and theft. Never mind those crimes were committed by the white mob.

Shortly after arriving at his brother's house in Independence, local police, at the request of Tulsa authorities, paid a visit to Stradford. Asked if he would turn himself in, he replied, "Hell, no." Arrested and booked, he called his son in Chicago. Cornelius Stradford, a graduate of Columbia University Law School, took the first train to Kansas and posted the $6,500 (2013 value) bond. J. B. was told to stay put and appear in court on June 10. Convinced he would not get a fair trial if returned to Tulsa, Stradford and his son boarded the next train to Chicago. Incensed Tulsa litigators vowed to extradite and try him for the charge of inciting a riot.

Wrangling successfully against the extradition attempts, the aging Stradford settled into Chicago life with his wife, son, and numerous grandchildren. Trying to re-create his success in Tulsa, he practiced law and filed a suit in September against the American Central Insurance Company, trying to recover some of his real estate losses. Stradford did not appear at the hearing. Due to the riot exclusion clause in insurance policies and local leaders defining the travesty as a "riot," all riot victims' claims, including the one by the gentleman considered by some as an outlaw, were knocked out in legal fights.

Desiring to re-create his real estate prowess, he formed a group of investors to build a luxury hotel like the Stradford. Regrettably, the project ran out of money and the building was not completed. He did, however, construct a candy store, barbershop, and a small pool hall. His modest business holdings in Chicago reminded him of what once was.

Stradford lost more than money in the Tulsa Race Riot of 1921. He lost his black sense of place. In his unpublished memoirs, he wrote, "It is incredible to believe that in this civilized age that a white man could be so void of humanity." He continued, "My soul cried for revenge and prayed for the day to come when I could personally avenge the wrongs which had been perpetrated against me." He died in 1935 at the age of 74. Sixty years later, family members extracted his atonement.

––––––––––––

Cornelius E. Toole was a former NAACP lawyer and a Cook County, Illinois, circuit court judge. He was also a great-grandson of J. B. Stradford. Toole harbored resentment for the smearing of his relative's name, the destroying of his properties and his dreams. Through impassioned communications with Mayor Susan Savage and local black leader Don Ross in 1996, the 63-year-old former judge insisted that the charges against Stradford be dismissed. The decision rested on the shoulders of first-year District Attorney Bill LaFortune who needed to render an opinion on a strict legal question—did evidence support the notion that Stradford incited a riot?

Nancy Little was assigned the investigation. Her detailed inspection revealed innocent black families suffered a ruthless attack. She was shocked. While it was undeniable Stradford violated law by jumping bail and refusing extradition, Little concluded he was innocent of inciting a riot. LaFortune vacated the charges.

In October of 1996, Stradfords from Texas, Illinois, Ohio, and New York set foot in Oklahoma—the first time since June of 1921. The vindication ceremony at the Greenwood Cultural Center featured moving statements from Governor Frank Keating. Quite simply, District Attorney Bill LaFortune presented the motion to dismiss and Judge Jesse Harris accepted it.

John the Baptist Stradford was the first riot victim indicted and the last alleged outlaw exonerated—first charged, last freed.

THE TIGER KING UNTAMED

Joe Exotic is a model, a magician, and a country music singer. And, according to animal welfare advocates, he's a lynchpin in the exotic animal trade.

By *Holly Wall*

"HANG ON, I'm gonna go out there and throw up."

Near the end of our first hour-long interview, Joe Exotic, a.k.a. Joe Schreibvogel, interrupted my question and hoofed toward the gift shop's back door, his shoulder-length, bleach-blond mane waving at me beneath a beige ball cap. While I waited, I browsed the wares for sale around me. There were the typical stuffed animals and animal-themed tchotchkes you'd expect to find at the zoo, but there were some unexpected things as well: lion bobbleheads, for instance, available with or without tiny dachshunds perched on their paws. Tiger posters framed in cheap plastic. Hormel microwaveable meals. Bumper stickers with a mischievous-looking Calvin character in a backwards cap looking over his shoulder, sending a stream of urine onto the letters "PETA" or "HSUS."

There was an entire wall of brightly colored and patterned men's thong and brief underwear, some shimmery, all bearing the label "Tiger King." Beside them, more Tiger King products: soaps, lotions, and premium condoms. Next to those were CDs with Joe Exotic's name and picture on them, country music he recorded and burned himself. A couple of televisions inside the shop played his music videos on a loop.

Schreibvogel came back in after a couple of minutes, while I was still examining the premium condoms. Each label bore a photo of Joe wearing a shimmering zebra-print shirt, posing next to a tiger in front of a cascading waterfall.

"I took so many pain pills last night trying to get to sleep I made myself sick to my stomach," he said.

"Oh," I said. "Are you injured?"

"I hurt my back two days ago," he told me, his mouth growing drier as he spoke. "I ended up in the emergency room, and they gave me some pain pills, but they're just not working for me. I'm not a pill person."

Joe at the zoo on a weekday morning looked different from the Joe pictured on his Tiger King-branded candy and lotion. The sequined shirt, unbuttoned to his belly on the label, had been replaced with a camouflage thermal and a tan work shirt; white jeans traded for brown overalls. His mullet was hidden beneath a ball cap and his eyes behind a pair of dark sunglasses. He's tall and thin, with three stainless steel rings in his right ear, two in his left, and one barely hanging onto his left eyebrow. Permanent eyeliner is drawn around his eyes, and a horseshoe mustache frames his mouth. He has several tattoos, including a tiger on the right side of his chest, a peacock on the left, and three bullet holes, dripping blood, on his chest and stomach.

Joe founded the Garold Wayne Interactive Zoological Park, formerly the G.W. Exotic Animal Memorial Park, in 1999. It's named for his brother, Garold Wayne (everyone called him "G.W.") Schreibvogel, who died in a car accident in 1997. G.W. was moving his sister to Florida from Arlington, Texas, when a drunk driver, behind the wheel of a semi-truck, struck and killed him. After his brother's death, Schreibvogel sold the Arlington pet store they owned together and used those funds to build the zoo's first cages, placing them on land paid for by his parents with insurance money from a settlement with the trucking company.

Schreibvogel opened the park with a deer and a mountain lion, and he says his father asked him over and over, "Where are you going to get the animals to open this place?" Schreibvogel didn't have to look very hard; they came to him in herds. Lions, tigers, and other big cats; bears and monkeys; birds and reptiles.

Today, Schreibvogel claims the park has more than 800 animals spanning 128 species; the United States Department of Agriculture's most recent inventory, counted during a routine inspection and available online, puts it at 199, including 79 tigers, 16 lions, 14 grey wolves, 16 North American black bears, and 10 species of nonhuman primates.[1]

Some of them, Schreibvogel claims, were rescued from derelict owners; others were "re-homed," the term he uses when he means an animal wasn't in danger, but its owner couldn't afford—or didn't want—to take care of it anymore.

———————

Kuo Wei Lee, a housing developer from Plano, had gotten into the emu business in 1995, just as the bubble was about to burst. The emu craze hit Texas hard in the early '90s, when a breeding pair of birds fetched some $50,000. Thousands of ranchers flocked to the business, sure that low-cholesterol emu steaks would replace beef at grocery store butcher counters and restaurant tables, and that emu oil would fly off of health food store shelves as a veritable cure-all.

But consumers didn't demand emu products like promoters thought they would, and by 1999, when Joe Schreibvogel traveled to Red Oak, Texas, about 20 miles south of Dallas, with two other rescue volunteers, police officers, and high school members of the Future Farmers of America to rescue more than 100 starving, emaciated emus, the birds were virtually worthless—though still terribly expensive. A flock could cost up to $4,000 to feed and house, so ranchers simply stopped feeding

———————

1 It's hard to tell whose count is accurate. Carole Baskin, founder of Big Cat Rescue in Tampa, Florida, has said: "As a facility licensed by USDA, Big Cat Rescue is regularly inspected; through these inspections I have learned of the deficiencies in USDA oversight of exhibition facilities. For example, it appears to be routine practice for USDA exhibitors to simply ask licensees for an inventory of their animals, as opposed to personally verifying these numbers." On top of that, animals frequently move into and out of the park. Between November 14, 2013, and March 10, 2014, for example, the park's inventory was down by 18 tigers and up by 11 North American black bears. Also, the USDA does not count birds or reptiles in its inventories, because they are not protected by the Animal Welfare Act.

them—or, as Lee explained to authorities, fed them only intermittently, sometimes spacing their meals weeks apart, in an attempt to make the feed last.

Schreibvogel didn't have any experience with emus. He'd rescued native species through his Arlington pet store, and was just beginning to dabble in exotics. But he'd heard about the emus, and he wanted to help. He planned to take the birds back to Wynnewood,[2] where he was just getting his zoo up and running.

The two-day rescue went horribly awry, according to both Schreibvogel and newspaper reports of the incident. Fifteen birds died from the stress of the event, most of them trampled to death by their kin, and Schreibvogel shot another six—with shotguns borrowed from the local police force—to save them from the same fate. Some were killed instantly; others flopped and jumped around before they died.

"We saved over 100 birds, and we sacrificed the last… so they would not go through what that one did," Schreibvogel told a reporter from the *Dallas Morning News*, pointing to a bird who'd died while being wrangled.

A grand jury convened to investigate Schreibvogel's handling of the emu rescue declined to deliver an indictment, and Schreibvogel never took the birds home to Wynnewood. They stayed, instead, according to newspaper reports, with a rancher in Tolar, Texas, who promised to bring them back to health and then find them permanent homes. Schreibvogel sued the Dallas Society for the Prevention of Cruelty to Animals for defamation, saying its actions during the rescue—it released a videotape of the emu roundup to local reporters—led to a loss of business at his Arlington pet store.

It was only his first fight with an animal rights agency.

---

2 Pronounced "Winnie-wood."

The Garold Wayne Interactive Zoological Park sits on 45 acres on a narrow road just off of Interstate 35, about an hour south of Oklahoma City. A path leading toward a wooden, Western saloon-looking structure that houses the gift shop and park entrance is lined with signs that alternately urge visitors to donate money to the park and warn them to enter at their own risk.

Above the entrance, a large sign welcomes guests to the Garold Wayne Interactive Zoological Park. Underneath that, in smaller letters, "Accredited by The USZA.[3]" Admission to the zoo is $15. Guided tours are $35, and playtime with a tiger cub costs $45. For $25, you can buy a bag of raw chicken and feed the big cats. Prices and tour times are displayed behind the front desk and surrounded by autographed photos of celebrities—Pierce Brosnan, Bill Cosby, John Herrington, and Clint Black, to name just a few.

Beyond the gift shop, dirt pathways cut through expanses of grass, leading visitors alongside tall metal cages, inside of which tigers pace, bears wrestle, and monkeys—one of them, at least—gnaw on fat, striped peppermint sticks. The place smells faintly of manure, a scent detectable from the gravel parking lot, where the low roars of caged tigers welcome you to Wynnewood.

Adorning most of the cages are signs dedicating them and the animals inside of them to the memory of someone who has died. "Every cage is a memorial to someone," Schreibvogel told me. "The animals get to live in honor of people who've passed away.

"We actually have three people who are buried under their memorials."

The park is split into two sections: at the front are, according to Joe's count, 500 animals—big cats, bears, monkeys, porcupines, hyenas, a

---

3 The United States Zoological Association's mailing address matches the G.W.'s Zoo's physical address, and information on its website mimics that of the zoo's.

camel, and a skunk. Visitors can wander this area on their own, stopping by the tiki lounge for a cocktail or soda pop, letting their kids play in a large sandbox, or taking in a magic show at one of the newly built stages. Free-range chickens, ducks, and geese wander this part of the park, too. As he guides me through the park, Schreibvogel stops to scratch a camel's head, kiss a lion, baby-talk to the animals.

The back half of the park requires the guidance of a park employee. There are no barriers between the cages and the pathway in this section of the park, which houses 82 big cats, 23 wolves,[4] and a zebu, and the animals back here are warier of humans.

Outside the door to Schreibvogel's home—he and all nine of his employees live on the zoo's premises—a tiger named Brutus paces in one cage, and a lion named Bonedigger runs around with four dachshunds in another. Both big cats, as well as the dogs, were born and raised at the zoo. Inside the house, Schreibvogel and his husbands live with three liliger cubs, a baby white tiger,[5] two more dachshunds, a capuchin monkey, and a baboon.

Schreibvogel wasn't always interested in exotic animals; that was his brother's passion. They were raised in Wyoming and kept porcupines, antelope, raccoons, and the like, and began dabbling in exotic animals at their pet store in Texas.

"But my brother's big fantasy in life was to go to Africa and see the jungle," Schreibvogel said, "the real animals running around wild. And since he died before that happened, that's kind of why we took the exotic approach, to rescue exotic animals, because he just always wanted to go to Africa and see them in their natural habitat."[6]

Schreibvogel's mom, Shirley, helps out around the park. His father, Francis, would, but he was recently diagnosed with Alzheimer's. Schreibvogel has two sisters and a brother he hasn't spoken to in 17 years, not since G.W. died. Schreibvogel said they thought the money from

---

4 According to Schreibvogel's count.
5 All big cat cubs live in Schreibvogel's home while they're on the bottle. They move outside when they're about three or four months old.
6 During the emu rescue, Schreibvogel told a reporter with the *Dallas Morning News* that his brother's "lifetime dream was to go to Australia."

the insurance settlement, around $140,000, should have been divided among the four of them, not spent on the zoo. "It was just plain greed," he told me.

Schreibvogel's two husbands, John Finlay and Travis Maldonado, both of whom he wed in January,[7] also work at the park—in fact, he met them here.

Before he opened the park, and before he and his brother ran the pet shop in Arlington, Schreibvogel was the police chief of Eastvale, Texas, a small municipality in Denton County that consolidated with The Colony in 1987.

He's had four heart attacks.

He's a country music singer and songwriter—he's released two albums independently and made several music videos—and a model. He's got his own personal line of candy, underwear, and toiletries. He performs a Copperfield-style stage illusion show, sometimes using small animals as props,[8] and he airs a nightly web show called JoeExoticTV.

Recently, he told me, he signed a deal with a major cable station to film a reality show at the park, and he hired a New York PR firm to work with Paris Hilton on a personal line of cologne.

And, according to the Humane Society of the United States, he's a lynchpin in the country's exotic animal trade. According to veterinary reports, between February 19, 2011, and September 5, 2013, he transferred at least 51 tigers, seven lions, two leopards, five bears, and two monkeys to facilities outside of Oklahoma. In 2013 alone, he transported nearly 21 tigers cubs. And at least two of his lions went to a facility in Illinois known for slaughtering them.

---

7   At the time of this writing, neither gay marriage nor polygamy was legal in Oklahoma, but Schreibvogel refers to the ceremony, attended by about 100 people, as a wedding and his partners as husbands. And he says no one in or around his small town has criticized or said anything negative to him about it.

8   Schreibvogel used to use tigers in his magic show, but he stopped amid protests from animal welfare activists.

It's widely reported that there are more tigers in captivity than there are in the wild[9] and that there are more exotic animals living in people's backyards than there are in zoos. In most states, it's legal.[10]

Until this year, citizens of Ohio could own any animal they wanted. They didn't need a permit, and they weren't required to inform their neighbors if they had a potentially deadly animal in their backyard. That changed on January 1, 2014—now, no exotic animals are allowed to be brought into the state by private owners[11]; owners of the ones already there must obtain a permit to keep them.

The change in Ohio's law happened as a result of an incident in Zanesville one October night in 2011. Terry Thompson, who lived with his wife, Marian, and 56 exotic species, released the animals from their pens—including 18 tigers, 17 lions, eight bears, three cougars, and two wolves—before killing himself. Authorities in Zanesville said they had no choice but to shoot the animals they came in contact with. The hunt lasted all night and into the morning, and 49 animals were killed.

Some of Thompson's defenders, including Schreibvogel, who lobbied against Ohio's Dangerous Wild Animal Act, allege that Thompson's so-called suicide was a cover-up; he was actually murdered, they say, by animal rights activists who want to ban private ownership of exotics altogether.

In 2012, the Humane Society of the United States called the G.W. Zoo a "ticking time bomb, potentially 10 times worse than Zanesville."

---

9 One estimation puts that number at 5,000, and most of those are kept by private owners, not zoos.

10 Only 21 states ban exotic animal ownership, and most of those laws concern big cats, bears, wolves, primates, and reptiles. Other states have a "partial ban," allowing ownership of some exotic animals but not others. Eight states have no regulations regarding exotic animal ownership, and, in 13, a permit or a license is required.

11 Exempted are sanctuaries, research institutions, and facilities accredited by the Association of Zoos and Aquariums and the Zoological Association of America.

Schreibvogel, in response, told CBS News: "It is a ticking time bomb. If somebody thinks they're going to walk in here and take my animals away, it's going to be a small Waco."

Oklahoma is one of the 13 states where individuals are permitted to own exotic animals. The only stipulation is that they must acquire a commercial wildlife breeder's license, whether they intend to breed the animals or not. The license costs $48 and is issued "to any person whom the director believes to be acting in good faith."

People who intend to exhibit their animals to the public must be licensed by the USDA and are governed only by that agency, which sends inspectors out to look routinely for violations of the Animal Welfare Act. The USDA has no jurisdiction over exotic animal owners—or private sanctuaries—that don't exhibit their animals.

Some animal welfare advocates argue that the difference between sanctuaries and zoos is that sanctuaries don't exploit their animals by exhibiting them to the public like zoos do.[12]

Schreibvogel disagrees: "In my opinion, if you're not licensed by the USDA and you're not open to the public, you are an animal hoarder that found out that [by] filing 501(c)3, you can get the public to fund your hobby. That's what 90 percent of them are."

But Schreibvogel isn't just giving exotic animals a place to live out the rest of their lives; he's also buying, selling, trading, and breeding them.

In February of 2014, the Humane Society of the United States, The Fund for Animals, the International Fund for Animal Welfare, Born Free USA, and Big Cat Rescue filed a petition with the USDA, urging the agency to permanently revoke Schreibvogel's exhibitor license.

---

12 The Global Federation for Animal Sanctuaries, an accrediting organization, says "a sanctuary is a facility that rescues and provides shelter and care for animals that have been abused, injured, abandoned or are otherwise in need" and there can be "no commercial trade, no invasive or intrusive research, no unescorted public visitation or contact, and no removal of wild animals for exhibition, education, or research."

Much of the evidence used against Schreibvogel came from an undercover investigation of the facility and from his own website and YouTube channel—there was a video of Schreibvogel stitching a large, deep wound on a lioness, saying he'd already stitched the same wound several times; one of a dachshund licking a lion's teeth; and one of a tiger named Gabriel, who'd allegedly been bitten by a rattlesnake, dragged into his den, and forced to drink from a hose. Gabriel vomited at least once and was found dead the next morning. The organizations also pointed to a mauling that occurred in October 2013—an employee put her arm in a tiger cage and lost part of it[13]—as evidence of Schreibvogel's failure to properly train employees.

The Humane Society conducted an undercover investigation at the G.W. Zoo in the summer and fall of 2011, and its subsequent report alleged the park to be "a commercial operation—that often seeks donations for 'rescued' animals—that endangers both animals and the public along with possibly violating federal and state laws and regulations."

Among several claims, HSUS alleged that cubs were "punched, dragged, and hit with whips during 'training'; visitors, including children, were bitten, scratched, and knocked down by tiger cubs." The HSUS report also claimed five endangered tigers, three federally protected hawks, six baby skunks, one adult skunk, five baby raccoons, one adult raccoon, a coatimundi, a parakeet, a baby peacock, a goose, a groundhog, a rabbit, and an iguana all died during the investigation, sometimes under mysterious or gruesome circumstances. The report also offered a gory account of a horse being shot five times, and a one-eyed bobcat being "destroyed."

---

13 This March, the Occupational Safety and Health Administration released the findings of its investigation into the incident, determining "the employer houses exotic animals such as bears and felids. Protective barriers were not provided around feeding chutes, the area around the gates used to access felid and bear enclosures, and the area around the opening to the catch pens used for felids and bears." OSHA fined Schreibvogel $2,400 (reduced from the original proposed fine of $5,200). The employee who was injured still works at the park.

The HSUS isn't the only organization to investigate the park; in 2006, People for the Ethical Treatment of Animals sent someone in to work undercover from February to June. PETA's report is more detailed than HSUS', but the sentiment is similar. Some of the allegations include:

- Two healthy adult tigers were killed, and their teeth were cut out to be given away as gifts before their carcasses were dumped into a reeking, festering garbage pit.
- Two badly injured horses in excruciating pain, including a former racehorse with a broken leg, were dumped at GW, and staff let them suffer for days until they could be butchered.
- Tigers attacked a lion and chewed off her leg. When she pulled out the stitches, her open wound went untreated. Although she moaned for weeks, she was given nothing for pain. ...
- Employees were instructed to falsify USDA-required paperwork regarding feeding schedules and environmental enrichment for primates to cover up the fact that animals went hungry for days at a time and that the psychological well-being of primates was not being met.

Both organizations ended their investigations by asking the USDA—and, in HSUS' case, the U.S. Fish & Wildlife Services and the Oklahoma Department of Wildlife Conservation—to investigate possible Animal Welfare Act and other animal cruelty violations.

Two former employees also filed complaints with the USDA. One, Ryan Olszta, who worked as the educational director at the G.W. Zoo from December of 2012 to January of 2013, told the USDA in his complaint—and me, by phone—that he saw juvenile tigers kicked in the face and thrown into the air; adult tigers choked, kicked, and hit with a rod; and staff threatened and abused. Olszta also told me he saw Schreibvogel and Finlay smoking meth and found the drug and paraphernalia in their room.

The USDA currently has three open investigations at G.W. Zoo, although a spokesperson for the agency declined to elaborate on what exactly the USDA is investigating.[14] What the Humane Society claims is most troubling is that Schreibvogel is supplying tiger cubs to other "substandard parks" and zoos around the country, perpetuating more animal abuse and the need for true rescue sanctuaries to house an ever-growing population of aging large cats.

———————

Part of the G.W. Zoo's business involves breeding tigers and other big cats and allowing park visitors to play with the cubs. Anna Frostic, staff attorney for HSUS, says Schreibvogel is taking advantage of a loophole within the Animal Welfare Act that prevents the public from interacting with large cats younger than eight weeks and older than 12 weeks, providing him with a four-week window to charge the public between $25 and $55 to pet, play with, and interact with tiger cubs. The service is still available on the park's premises, but Schreibvogel shuttered an operation that was taking him to malls around the country, sometimes performing magic shows, almost always charging the public for a once-in-a-lifetime opportunity: to interact with a cute, cuddly tiger cub.

In 2012, the Humane Society of the United States, the World Wildlife Fund, the Global Federal of Animal Sanctuaries, the International Fund for Animal Welfare, Born Free USA, The Fund for Animals, Big Cat Rescue, and the Detroit Zoological Society petitioned the USDA to enact a rule that would prohibit the public from interacting with big cats, bears, and non-human primates at zoos and parks like Schreibvogel's.[15]

The petitioning groups wrote: "Animals subjected to public contact exhibition (many endangered) are irresponsibly bred with no regard for genetic integrity; they are prematurely and forcibly separated from their mothers and deprived of normal biological and behavioral de-

———————

14 According to a USDA spokesperson, one of the open investigations began in 2010, one in 2012, and one in 2013. The USDA has investigated the G.W. Zoo a total of eight times since 2003. In 2006, the USDA found the park guilty of several Animal Welfare Act violations, suspended operations for two weeks, and fined Schreibvogel $25,000.

15 According to the petition, public interaction with exotic animals is a "lucrative trend" in at least 70 parks and zoos around the country.

velopment; they are subjected to excessive handling that poses a risk to the health of undeveloped animals and to the safety of humans (especially children) interacting with them; they often travel the country in cramped enclosures for the commercial gain of licensees; and they are often disposed of at substandard facilities when they are no longer commercially useful."

Schreibvogel said he stopped Tigers in Need, his traveling cub show, more than two years ago, not because of the constant opposition by animal rights advocates, but because he couldn't find enough dependable help.

"When I decided to stop that, we were on a 42-week tour in 2010—nope, 2011. And I finished it with 17 days in Las Vegas, and I chased my employees around Las Vegas every day," he said. "Drunk. They would come in when it was time to go to work—they were just coming in from that night. And when I got home, I parked my semis and I ain't moved them since. And, you know, I just enjoy being home more now."

Schreibvogel does admit to breeding his tigers, but said he only produces about seven cubs a year—a notion Frostic was quick to refute, pointing to an incident in 2010 when 23 tiger cubs died over a period of seven months, Schreibvogel said, because of bad kitten formula.[16] Schreibvogel frequently posts photos to his Facebook page of new litters of big cat and bear cubs and wolf pups, and, according to counts by former park employees, the number of tiger cubs and other animal babies born at the zoo far exceeds seven a year.

Schreibvogel said his park was the first one in the country to produce liliger cubs—a cross between a lion and a liger—as well as taliger cubs, the offspring of a tiger and a liger.

"I work real close with Texas A&M University, with their genetic scientists,[17]" Schreibvogel told me as we toured the park on a cold, wet day in February. The ground was dotted with piles of melting snow and squished beneath our feet. "And, you know, there are so many places

---

16 The Food and Drug Administration tested samples of the formula provided by Schreibvogel and found no traces of salmonella or *Cronobacter sakazakii.*

17 A genetics professor at A&M who said he knew Joe did not want to be quoted for this story.

out there, sanctuaries—and I hate the word 'sanctuary,' because most of them are just scams —but so many of them out there are sucking donations and money out of the public getting them to think white tigers are inbred and that's the only way you can get white tigers and so on and so forth.[18] So we started 12, 13 years ago with our first ligers. And what ligers done was proved that, genetically, a tiger and a lion are the same animal or they could not reproduce. So we got healthy ligers, and then we did so many DNA and genetic tests and all of our white tigers and proved none of them are related, so they're not inbred to be white. So the big myth was, are ligers sterile? So we put a liger female with a lion male and let them grow up together so they knew each other and had the first litter of liligers.[19] So now we've proved that cross-breeds are not sterile and can produce healthy offspring as well."

The Association of Zoos and Aquariums, which accredits the Tulsa and Oklahoma City zoos, opposes captive breeding outside of its Species Survival Plan, which employs teams of biologists, geneticists, and ecologists to determine which animals of a specific species would be best suited to maintain the genetic integrity of their species. The ultimate goal of this breeding plan is to have the capability to reintroduce a species into the wild, should circumstances ever become that dire.

Dr. Ronald Tilson, a tiger husbandry expert who coordinated the AZA's Tiger Species Survival Plan from 1987 to 2011, told the USDA: "Breeding practices by public contact exhibitors… seriously undermine legitimate in-situ species conservation efforts, jeopardize animal health

---

18. According to the Association of Zoos and Aquariums, white tigers are indeed the product of intentional inbreeding. "Most white tigers currently in captivity are Amur-Indian hybrids that have been highly inbred to achieve continued occurrence of the colormorph," the association stated in a paper available on its website. "…In the case of the white tiger one recessive allele has to come from each parent to allow for expression of the white striped color morph. While this has happened rarely in wild tiger populations, such as one in India many decades ago, and may occur in wild populations of various species occasionally (e.g., white deer, lion, ferret), such traits only rarely get expressed, and, when expressed, it is very likely that they confer a disadvantage resulting in reduced fitness for a given individual under most circumstances."

19 Three cubs, all female.

and welfare issues, and send false and misleading conservation messages to the general public."

The problem with breeding isn't just in the practice itself, opponents argue; once the cubs are too old for the public to interact with, they're often transferred to other "substandard" facilities.[20] And commercial breeding, Frostic said—as well as allowing the public to interact with cubs—feeds the demand for private ownership of exotic animals, which, in turn, further endangers the species still living in the wild.

"The evidence we have shows that when people have the opportunity to cavort around with babies of endangered species, it doesn't make them want to run out and donate money to a conservation campaign; it increases people's desire to keep animals as exotic pets," Frostic said. "It perpetuates the cycle of breeding to facilitate that demand."

On top of that, with the number of tigers being born into captivity in this country—and no clear count of what that number actually is—there's no guarantee that some of them aren't ending up in the very lucrative international parts trade.

"If what's happening in captivity in the U.S. is fueling the trade in tiger parts internationally, that is exactly what is threatening the species in the wild," Frostic said.

Several organizations, including HSUS and Big Cat Rescue, have signed on to support federal legislation that would ban private possession and breeding of big cats. "If that passes, over the next decade, the captive population of generic tigers—not pure subspecies—would die out and Carole and I could focus all of our effort where it should be, on saving cats in the wild," Howard Baskin, advisory board chairman of Big Cat Rescue in Tampa, Florida, wrote to me in an email. "I believe that if all the money spent in this country to keep big cats in inappropriate, tiny, barren cages were spent stopping the poaching and preserving the habitat in the wild, we could keep these cats from going extinct in the wild."

Howard's wife, Carole Baskin, founded Big Cat Rescue in 1992. The couple, whose facility once bred big cats itself, are two of Schreib-

---

20. According to HSUS' Anna Frostic, AZA-accredited zoos never get their animals from private commercial breeders.

vogel's most vocal opponents, even going as far as to sue Schreibvogel for violating their copyrights and other intellectual property rights. Schreibvogel has accused Big Cat Rescue and the Humane Society of the United States of being in cahoots, with the ultimate objective of getting "all of the big cats out of every zoo and sanctuary and moved out to their place by the year 2025."[21]

"As long as I'm in business, and I'm breeding tigers, I screw their 25-year plan," Schreibvogel said. He said that all of their efforts—the petitions, the press releases—are aimed at putting him out of business. "But unfortunately I'm not the type of person that's just going to roll over and play dead for them. So I fight back."

The fight with Big Cat Rescue started in 2010. At the time, Schreibvogel was traveling with Tigers in Need, exhibiting tiger cubs and allowing members of the public, for a fee, to play and have photos taken with them.

"For years it has been part of our advocacy work to oppose exploitation of cubs for petting, photo ops, and swimming," Howard Baskin told me via email. "Prior to 2010 that work was done by Carole, our founder, my wife. When she found a traveling cub display, she would email our supporters asking them to email—or a few might call on the phone—and politely express to the venue why this was a miserable life for the cubs and show them that while they may see people come to the venue to do the petting, i.e. draw customers, what they did not see is all the people who love animals and did not want to see this mistreatment."

Schreibvogel said Carole Baskin's opposition started in 2006 and that he "pretty much ignored" it until 2010, but it got "worse and worse." She'd send press releases out about him, post on Facebook, and any time his traveling cub act showed up at a mall, it was met with protesters. Schreibvogel called her "obsessed."

---

21 Both Frostic, of the Humane Society, and Howard Baskin called Schreibvogel's accusation "ridiculous."

So, in 2010, Schreibvogel said, he started fighting back, posting his own accusations about Big Cat Rescue on his website and Facebook, airing those accusations on his web show, JoeExoticTV, and sending out his own press releases, many of them attacking Carole Baskin personally. Then he changed the name of his traveling show to Big Cat Rescue Entertainment. He said it was to streamline his marketing materials, but the Baskins argued he was trying to create confusion between the two organizations, and they sued him for copyright infringement. They also sued him for violation of intellectual property rights, accusing him of "using, altering, and/or mischaracterizing" photos and videos that belonged to Big Cat Rescue.

Schreibvogel counter sued for slander and libel; the judge threw out his claims in a motion for summary judgment.

Before the case went to trial, Schreibvogel agreed to a Consent Final Judgment, and Big Cat Rescue was awarded nearly $1 million. Then Schreibvogel filed for bankruptcy protection, both personally and on behalf of the park. He said, after spending $280,000, he ran out of money to defend himself. The park's bankruptcy was dismissed, but his personal bankruptcy is still pending.

Prior to filing bankruptcy, Schreibvogel transferred the deed to the land to his mother and shuttered the G.W. Exotic Animal Foundation, the 501(c)3 nonprofit operating the G.W. Exotic Animal Memorial Park. The park then resumed operation under a new name—the Garold Wayne Interactive Zoological Park—incorporated under three of his employees. The Baskins allege that the assets of the old zoo were improperly transferred to the new zoo.

"The staff members wanted to incorporate a new zoo to save the animals," Schreibvogel told me. Those employees—John Reinke, Tracy Schultz, and John Finlay (one of Joe's husbands)—are still operating under Schreibvogel's USDA license, but he said he's working to get them one of their own.

Schreibvogel denies owning or running the park. "I'm not on the board; I don't wanna be on the board. I don't wanna own a zoo."

"Right now," he said, "I am just the entertainment."

In the four months since HSUS and others filed the petition asking the USDA to revoke Schreibvogel's license, more bad news has hit the zoo.

In March, a female chimpanzee named Bongo was found dead on the floor of her cage. Schreibvogel said she likely had a heart attack and that he tried to give her CPR, but PETA sent out a press release and called for the USDA to investigate. "Joe Schreibvogel's facility is a deathtrap for animals," PETA spokesperson Delcianna Winders said. A couple of days later, two birds were found dead in their cages. PETA's press release said photos of the birds, which Schreibvogel posted to his Facebook page, showed evidence of starvation and neglect. Schreibvogel blamed PETA, accusing an employee of working undercover for the organization and starving the birds intentionally, just to make him look bad.

"See, every day, all of our food containers come out of the commissary in special little plastic containers for that day. We found every one of them under the fucking couch in the bird building," Schreibvogel said. "He purposely didn't feed them. And it's a big place to keep track of, but you can only do so much."

Schreibvogel said he explained Bongo's situation to the USDA inspector, who seemed to understand, but in mid-May, the agency issued the zoo a citation for failure to provide adequate veterinary care to a black bear that was wounded by another black bear. According to the inspection report, a vet sutured the wound, but it dehisced. Schreibvogel tried to close it, but it was found open and bleeding again. The bear languished for 10 days before the park and the vet decided to euthanize it. The USDA didn't fine the zoo, but a spokesman for PETA, which sent out a press release about the citation, said it could "be used to support future enforcement action by the USDA against the exhibitor."

Schreibvogel issued his own press release, saying PETA has taken "some drastic measures to tarnish the image of local zoos like The Garold Wayne Interactive Zoological," blaming PETA, in effect, for the bear's death. The release goes on: "PETA's attitude to animal treatment has resulted in unfortunate incidents such as the latest incident where the zoo was compelled to euthanize a bear. Joe Exotic was personally involved in the treatment of the bear that was injured in a turf war. Joe had his treatment strategy all figured out but it was abruptly interrupted and stopped by PETA authorities, leading to the death of the animal."

Schreibvogel said the barrage of accusations against him are nothing more than attempts by his foes to raise money for themselves. "You know, I don't even have to know you. If I say that you beat your pug every day, and I'm trying to save your pug, whether I am or not, I could raise 2,000 bucks today trying to save your pug," Schreibvogel said. "So if they can make you look bad, people send them money. Because they think they're going to help my animals, when actually, in turn, they're doing nothing but hurting our funding."

Olszta told me: "I think Joe started out with the right intention. I think he truly did want to help animals at one point, back when he first started, and then it turned into the natural human want for money. I think money has changed him."

Another former employee, who worked at the park as recently as this year, has filed a new complaint with the USDA, alleging, among other things, that Schreibvogel used a shovel to kill a domestic cat, that he and his husbands ran over emus with ATVs, that birds and reptiles were inadequately fed, and that several wolf pups died without anyone investigating why.

Schreibvogel's response to the petitions and the accusations of abuse has been: "Come look. See for yourself." And, according to him, people have.

While the bad press has hurt the park's funding, Schreibvogel said it's also brought people to the park, people curious about what's happening there, people who wouldn't otherwise know where Wynnewood, Oklahoma, is or who Joe Exotic is. And Schreibvogel plans to use that to his advantage.

As soon as he gets his employees their own USDA license, "Joe is just going to Hollywood," he said.

"You bet, you bet. I get probably a TV show or a movie offer once a week. All because—well, that's where I've got to kind of thank the animal rights people, because nobody would know me if it weren't for them."

THIS IS MY BELOVED SON

How Richard Roberts went from being the chosen heir to his father's empire to a prodigal son ostracized from the kingdom.

By *Kiera Feldman*

Two Oral Roberts Ministries employees crouched on a desk on their hands and knees, their heads sticking through a hole in the wall. The voices of the Oral Roberts University Board of Regents on the speakerphone conference call one floor below carried up through the thin ceiling panels. Patriarch Oral Roberts was urging Richard, his successor, not to go on *Larry King Live* that evening.

"I think I should," they heard Richard tell his father. Oral thought Larry King would eat Richard alive.

A week earlier, a lawsuit hit the front pages of the *Tulsa World*, alleging that Richard and Lindsay Roberts, ORU's president and first lady since 1993, treated the university as a personal ATM. The university's finances were inadvertently cracked open by three professors who claimed they'd been fired for questioning Richard's efforts to involve ORU in campaigning for Senator Jim Inhofe's chosen candidate in Tulsa's mayoral election. What's more, the suit claimed Lindsay sent hundreds of text messages to "underage males" between the hours of 1 a.m. and 3 a.m. on cell phones expensed to the university.

ORU's Board of Regents agreed: *Larry King* was a terrible idea. John Hagee, Kenneth Copeland, Benny Hinn, Creflo Dollar—ORU's board was a who's who of televangelists. Oral was the original pioneer of television ministry. He trained up a whole generation of jet-setting mega-church pastors who preached the prosperity gospel: Plant a seed— meaning, send a check—and God will reward you with health, wealth, and happiness.

The eavesdroppers could tell Richard saw the writing on the wall. "There was no exonerating himself at that point," one remembers. "He just thought it would be cool to go on *Larry King*."

Richard had been like a moth to the limelight since childhood, when he began singing in his father's tent crusades. In the 1970s, at the height of Richard's celebrity as a Christian singer, he was starring in prime-time television specials with the likes of Johnny Cash and Robert Goulet, reaching tens of millions of viewers. With his signature streak of white hair and big, telegenic smile, Richard was most in his element when the cameras were rolling. If anyone ever asked if Richard was ready to perform, he'd fire back, "I was born ready."

And so Richard and Lindsay boarded the ORU jet and flew from Tulsa to New York. In the October 9, 2007, broadcast, Larry King listed just a few of the many allegations against the Robertses: remodeling their ORU-owned home 11 times in 14 years at university expense; forcing employees to do their daughters' homework; bestowing over a dozen ORU scholarships upon the children of their wealthy friends; the $39,000 Lindsay expensed in clothing at Chico's in a single year; the stable of horses ORU maintained for the Roberts daughters' exclusive use.

"Does it concern you that your excesses are so obvious that most people don't appear to be shocked to hear of them?" Larry King read aloud from an ORU alum's email. "I have not done anything wrong, Larry," Richard answered.

Off camera, Richard tried to rally the extended Roberts family in his defense. "We're all going to hang," Richard said (according to a niece's deposition). "We can either hang together or we can hang separately."

Meanwhile, the school was $52.5 million in debt. Campus was in shambles. The tiled steps leading up to the library were missing most of their tiles. Even the 200-foot-high Prayer Tower at the center of campus—the very symbol of the university, wrought from steel and tinted glass and resembling a gold-plated Space Needle—was rusting.

Still, hardly anyone knew just how bad things actually were. At this rate, in less than a fortnight the university would have to declare bankruptcy.

Oral, having retired to a condo in Newport Beach, returned to Tulsa for the first time in years. He moved back into "the compound"— the Roberts' six-house, nine-acre gated estate overlooking campus. At a chapel service, the much-beloved 89-year-old patriarch addressed students.

"The devil is not going to steal ORU," Oral promised.

The phone call came for Richard on Thanksgiving. Televangelist and ORU Regent Kenneth Copeland was on the line, according to a source who was present. That morning, another regent, Billy Joe Daugherty— one of Oral's protégés—faxed Copeland the receipts for the ORU jet. There was no denying Richard had been taking his family on lavish vacations and calling them "healing crusades," says the source.

"You're a damn fool. You should've paid the money," Copeland[1] told Richard, according to the source.

"I'm not supporting him," Copeland said to Oral. "Your son's out." (Copeland did not respond to a request for comment.)

Richard hung up the phone. He and his family were to be evicted from the compound—Richard's home of nearly five decades—his ties to ORU severed forever.

These were the terms: Mart Green, heir to the Hobby Lobby franchise of craft stores, would bail out the nearly bankrupt school with a pledge of $70 million—on condition of Richard's ouster. Richard would take with him his inheritance: the name Oral Roberts Ministries, where the checks get sent. In this way, the kingdom was divided.

---

1 Copeland was one to talk. Earlier that month, at the behest of Senator Charles Grassley, the Senate Finance Committee launched an investigation into the extravagant lifestyles of six prominent televangelists. Private jets, fancy cars, mansions—all paid for by their respective tax-exempt ministries. (Nonprofits are effectively taxpayer subsidized, and so personal enrichment through them is illegal.) Three of the six televangelists under investigation were ORU regents: Kenneth Copeland, Benny Hinn, and Creflo Dollar—the very people who'd been rubberstamping Richard's spending.

_____

"Success without a successor is failure," Oral often said. He dreamed that his brilliant first-born son, Ronnie, would succeed him. Yet, Ronnie refused the mantle, unwilling to play a role in the succession drama into which he'd been born. The eldest child, Rebecca, and the youngest, Roberta, were not considered suitable heirs: Only the sons would carry on the family name. It was Roberta alone among the Roberts children who was enchanted with the mythology of her father, the faith healer, and it was Roberta, a deeply studious child, who so loved the namesake school he built in South Tulsa, near the Arkansas River. But the house that Oral Roberts built had no room for daughters. That left Richard.

"Something Good Is Going to Happen to You" was Oral's slogan on TV. But a life lived on camera takes its toll.

Born in 1918, Oral Roberts was the son of an itinerant preacher in the Pentecostal Holiness Church—"Holycostal Penniless," kids in the church called it. When Oral's father was off preaching from town to town, sometimes the family would run out of money, and Oral and his mother would have to beg food from friends and neighbors. In the first half of the 20th century, Pentecostals were farmers, preachers, janitors, and rural teachers. Indelibly shaped and scarred by poverty, this was the movement that birthed the prosperity gospel in the latter half of the century.

In Pentecostalism, Oral is considered the godfather of the charismatic movement, which emphasizes divine miracles and ecstatic experience. Beginning in the late 1940s, Oral held crusades across the country and all over the world, his 10,000-person tent overflowing with those desperate for his touch to heal their suffering bodies and—often—finances. In the decades that followed, Oral turned faith healing into a wildly profitable enterprise. He hired top-notch admen and direct-mail consultants who perfected a method for using targeted mailings to solicit donations. The rate of return was so high that Oral's ministry had to get its own zip code.

Oral longed for middle-class respectability. Being a traveling faith healer and direct-mail mogul would never get him there. But brick and mortar would. When tent crusade audiences began to wane in the early 1960s, Oral switched gears and built a Pentecostal university, the first of its kind. From gold-tinted windows to golden latticework to the Prayer Tower's royal blue stripes and cherry red overhang, the entire campus glittered under the Oklahoma sun. "Nothing second-class for God," Oral liked to say.

Wayne Robinson, a former aide, grew up "Holycostal Penniless" as well. In his 1976 memoir, *Oral: The Warm, Intimate, Unauthorized Portrait of a Man of God*, Robinson depicts a fundamentally insecure person who spent a lifetime "constructing edifices which, once they are built, must be replaced by new structures—each time larger. Over and over again, these monuments declare, 'I ain't poor no more!' The *nouveau riche* tone of the ORU campus speaks of the poor boy who made it big. The gleaming gold is a reassuring renouncement of empty pockets and an empty stomach."

Oral was an absentee father, always off traveling the world on the tent crusade circuit. The few days a month when he actually was home, anything the family did or said was liable to end up incorporated into a television script. It was all "grist for the mill," remembers Robinson.

Of the four siblings, it was Richard who won his father's attentions, because Richard could be put to use: He could sing and he loved the stage. Plus, he was a jock; Oral needed a golf companion.

Richard never was much of a student. "He's allergic to books," Oral once explained. Richard began getting singing gigs at parties and pizza parlors around Tulsa, much to his parents' dismay. He idolized Frank Sinatra and Pat Boone and dreamed of heading to the nightclubs of Las Vegas or the stages of Broadway.

Richard spent the summer after high school at Interlochen, a prestigious performing arts camp on Lake Michigan. In the Interlochen production of *Annie Get Your Gun*, Richard landed the lead. He didn't talk much about being Oral Roberts' son—although everybody knew it. Once, a kid quoted Oral derisively, recalls Elliott Sirkin, another camper. "But that's not what he said," Richard responded quietly, clearly a little hurt. Otherwise, Richard seemed rather "cynical" about his father's ministry, remembers Allan Janus, another camper. But evidently Richard enjoyed the perks, like Oral's jet. "He would brag about how he could fly wherever," Janus recalls. Handsome, friendly, talented—Richard seemed to live a charmed life.

In the fall of 1966, Richard, dead-set against attending the newly opened ORU, headed for the University of Kansas instead. It was the best rebellion he could muster against his father. Out from under his parents' roof, he could smoke, drink, and chase girls—a tale of wayward youth that he has deployed again and again during his adult life, calling himself "the prodigal son." Home from college one break, father and son went golfing, according to Richard's well-worn account. Oral asked Richard to sing for him in an upcoming crusade.

"Look, Dad, just get off my back and get out of my life," Richard barked. "And don't you ever mention God to me again."

As Richard tells it, one day while taking a nap in his dorm at KU, he heard a voice that he assumed to be his roommate playing a joke on him. "You are in the wrong place," the voice said. Not once, but thrice. Richard checked under the bed, in the closet, everywhere. Nothing. Then he realized it was the Lord. "The Holy Spirit said to me, 'You are supposed to be at Oral Roberts University,'" Richard writes in a 2002 memoir, *Claim Your Inheritance*. "'That's where your destiny is.'"

A former ORU student recalls hearing Richard's mother, Evelyn, tell a slightly different version of that story: She and Oral went up to Kansas and summoned Richard back to the nest, wanting to keep an eye on him.

Richard's college rebellion proved to be short-lived. He flunked out. Singing, however, was different. His voice instructor, Harlan Jennings, remembers him as a highly disciplined and serious student, "one of the best I have taught over a long career."

The summer of 1967, between his freshman year at KU and his sophomore year at ORU, Richard successfully auditioned for a spot on the chorus at the Kansas City Starlight Theatre, an 8,000-seat venue on the regional circuit for Broadway stars. They put on *The Sound of Music* and *My Fair Lady* and *Westside Story* and more—77 shows in all, rehearsing all day and performing all night, seven days a week, with an extra 12 a.m.–5 a.m. rehearsal early Sunday morning. Richard worked like a dog, just like everyone else.

"I rented an apartment and lived like the devil all summer," Richard writes. It was, he says, "one last fling."

Starlight dancer Kitsey Plavcan was Richard's date to a party where Broadway singer (and later *Partridge Family* star) Shirley Jones made an appearance. Richard drove Plavcan home, and as she tells it, the evening did not end well. "He got drunk, and I was hanging out the door of the car, trying to find the line on the side of the road," she says. Just a few years later, she'd turn on the television, and there was Richard singing about Jesus on the Oral Roberts television show. "I used to sit there and laugh my fool head off at how wholesome he was," Plavcan remembers.

But in 1967, 18-year-old Richard found himself at a crossroads. Late at night, after a good deal of drinking, he'd say things like, "I'm not 100 percent sure about who I am, what I believe, what I believe about my father, is he real, is he all a fraud, is religion itself all a fraud," fellow chorus member Joe Warner recalls. In Christendom, everything would always be handed to Richard. The world beyond his father's kingdom was the great unknown.

Richard seemed resigned to his lot. He'd stay a Preacher's Kid forever—and not just any PK, but the son of Oral Roberts.

"Every PK has their own curse," says Warner. "But I think Richard's was greater than most."

Oral always conceived of his namesake university in opposition to the counterculture, an institution that would churn out clean-cut men and women in a time of middle-class anxiety over campus rebellion. Arriving on campus in 1965, the inaugural class of ORU students was united by a deep sense of purpose: Their job was to take Oral's vision of a healing God out into the world.

"It wasn't anything like going to college," writes Patti Holcombe. "It was more like founding a country."

Richard arrived at ORU in 1967 without that pioneering spirit. But he was soon drawn to Patti, a poised, feisty co-ed from Oregon with high cheekbones and a strong jaw line. They began to date, taking long walks, according to Patti's memoir, *Ashes to Gold*. "I'd like to sing on Broadway but only if it's God's will for me," he'd tell her. "All my life I've been Oral Roberts' son, but what about me? What about Richard? Why can't I have a life apart from my dad?"

Such a life apart would have to be wrought. "It all had to come to him, or Richard wasn't interested," remembers former ORU Regent Harry McNevin.

To join Oral's ministry, Richard needed a suitable wife. A good Christian girl, Patti fit the mold, although not quite as well as Richard's mother, Evelyn, who was even-tempered, graceful, and endlessly supportive of her husband's ambitions. "Patti has a mind of her own," people said, with varying degrees of admiration.

Shortly after the wedding, Oral called Richard and Patti into his study, sat down in an armchair by the fire, and began to cry. Oral said he'd had a dream: If either of them backslid—the term for leading an unchristian life, especially one outside Oral's domain—they'd be killed in a plane crash.

"It never occurred to us that maybe it wasn't God who had spoken," writes Patti, "but Oral trying to manipulate us to protect the ministry."

On the first night of their honeymoon, Patti wore a frilly lace nightgown, a gift from Evelyn. According to Patti, Richard looked up and said, "You know, you look fatter with your clothes off." They consummated their marriage in a coin-operated bed. Afterward, Patti says Richard put a quarter in the "Magic Fingers" contraption, making the bed vibrate and shake. Richard fell right asleep. The Magic Fingers kept Patti up for hours. They ate Thanksgiving dinner in the hotel. After a few days, they got bored and came home early from their honeymoon. So began their lives as "professional newlyweds," writes Patti.

Back at ORU, plans were soon underway for *Contact*, the first Oral Roberts prime-time television special. Oral was determined to make his telegenic son into a modern Christian celebrity. *Contact* (and its later incarnations in the 1970s) was a wholesome variety show with singing and dancing from the World Action Singers, a group of ORU students led by Richard. The show had flashy sets and costumes, solos by Richard and Patti, and a sermon from Oral. He had admen coin upbeat catchphrases like "Something Good Is Going to Happen to You."

Richard assumed the role of spoiled crown prince. Oral's men were instructed to give Richard small responsibilities to create the illusion of power. "Executive decisions," writes former producer Jerry Sholes in *Give Me That Prime-Time Religion*, "were made by other individuals who knew they were really reporting to Oral." Once, impatient with a television director, Richard turned to Sholes and snapped, "Is he a director or a pussy?" Sholes groaned. Richard didn't seem to care that ORU students—strict Christians—were within earshot. Richard had a golf date he wanted to get off to.

It was a struggle to get Richard to work a full day, say Oral's former aides. Richard was often MIA, and it was anyone's guess whether he was at the Tulsa Country Club or Southern Hills Country Club or elsewhere. "Sometimes we all had assignments to go get him to come home," remembers Al Bush, a close adviser of Oral's for decades. ("Richard was raised on a country club golf course," Bush once told the *Tulsa Tribune*. "If he's ever been hungry, it's because he overslept.")

According to Richard, he quit school after his junior year to work full-time for his father. According to Wayne Robinson, Oral's aide, the future ORU president flunked out of ORU. Either way, Richard was on the move. In March 1969, gospel singer Mahalia Jackson was the featured guest on the first *Contact* special, and 10 million people tuned in. Pat Boone, Richard's hero, followed as the featured guest on the second prime-time special.

"The golden age, we called it," remembers World Action Singer Larry Wayne Morbitt. They were reaching millions of the unchurched on prime time. ORU was swimming in cash in the 1970s, new campus buildings were going up, and the World Action Singers got to travel the world in luxury. For all his successes, however, Richard could not anticipate that he would face competition for his father's attentions.

A young black Pentecostal named Carlton Pearson, another World Action Singer, became Oral's protégé.

"[Richard] wanted to be perfect. He wanted to impress the people and to please his father," says Pearson. "More than God, I promise you. It wasn't about God," Pearson laughs.

In 1971, Oral brought Pearson into his office, where Richard was seated.

"Twenty-five percent of my income comes consistently from African-Americans," Oral said, according to Pearson. "Richard has the indispensable name of Roberts. He's my biological son. There's nothing you can do about that. But I need a black son. You are my black son."

Soon, Oral hired Pearson as associate evangelist, in large part to help groom Richard to take over the empire, Pearson says.

"I knew what Oral was thinking," says Pearson. "I want my son to succeed me like God's son pleased him. 'This is my beloved son, in whom I'm well pleased.'"

Richard still hadn't graduated college—he didn't get his BA from ORU until 1985, nearly 20 years after he began. But Oral added him to the ORU Board of Regents in 1971, at age 23. When fellow Regent Harry McNevin criticized Richard's plans to use the ORU jet for junkets, Richard declared that he would no longer attend any more meetings with him, according to McNevin. Before long, Oral made Richard vice president of Oral Roberts Evangelistic Association, the ministry.

As the years went on, Patti and others noticed Richard was becoming a clone of his father: how he spoke onstage, how he styled his hair. He recycled Oral's sermons verbatim. Oral had even given the couple their marriage bed.

"We slept in his bed," writes Patti, "and, in many ways, he slept in ours."

Patti readily admits she enjoyed the fruits of seed-faith ministry: glamorous vacations, expensive cars, shopping trips, jet-setting. But, according to her memoir, she grew increasingly uncomfortable with the resemblance seed-faith bore to the selling of indulgences prior to Martin Luther and the Reformation.

At an event in the mid 1970s, Patti happened to meet young Frank Schaeffer, son of the famous Christian philosopher and anti-abortion coalition builder Francis Schaeffer. Talking with Frank, Patti was relieved to find that they "were both angry with the superstar system of American religion," she writes. In her mind, Christian celebrity culture was pure idolatry. Frank heard Patti's concerns about her marriage and then counseled the couple.

Looking back, Frank remembers telling the couple that he eventually planned to make his own life, away from his paternal legacy, and they should too. This life, Frank said, was "poisonous." Richard nodded. "You're right, you're right, this is terrible. We need to get out," Richard said, according to Frank.

Oral's prophecy about Richard and Patti would prove to be slightly misdirected.

In 1977, Rebecca, Oral and Evelyn's eldest child, and her banker husband, Marshall Nash, were killed when, returning from their newly purchased condo in Aspen, their private plane went down over the cornfields of Kansas. Oral took his grief and made it into a television episode.

At first, Richard and Patti weren't able to conceive, and so they adopted a daughter. But soon Patti became pregnant. When she gave birth, she called Oral from the hospital. She apologized for not having a boy. "That doesn't matter," Oral assured her, according to aide Wayne Robinson. He would be proud of his granddaughter regardless, Oral said. He hung up the phone and turned to Robinson. "But it does matter," Oral confided.

To be on television with his father, Richard had to have it all—the lovely wife, the kids. People had to want to be them, as any ad-man knows. They were selling their image. It was "a corporate marriage," Patti writes, "designed not to upset the flow of dollars into the prized ministry."

Patti's ambitions began to exceed the family role into which she'd been cast: She wanted to have a singing career of her own. Oral warned Richard that he needed to get her under control, Patti recalls.

"I did not build this university or this ministry for you," Oral once told Patti, she recalls in *Ashes to Gold*. "I built it for Richard. You will never get to the top. It's not yours; it's Richard's."

Patti had become an unsuitable wife. One day, Richard came back from a fishing trip with his parents and announced they had given their permission to end the marriage. (Oral had a strict policy against employing divorcés, but he bent the rules for Richard.) After the divorce was finalized in early 1979, Patti writes, "Richard came into the bedroom and said, 'I'm so sorry our marriage didn't work out,' and extended his hand for me to shake."

With turmoil erupting in Christendom over the divorce, 30-year-old Richard quickly set about the business of finding another wife. Within a year, he married Linda "Lindsay" Salem, a 23-year-old Christian of Lebanese descent from Florida, who was attending ORU's law school. She had black hair and a heart-shaped face, cute but not regal like Patti.

Lindsay kept having miscarriages. Finally, she carried a baby to term. In 1984, Lindsay gave birth to a male heir. They named him Richard Oral Roberts. So much was riding on that baby. "Oh, how I wanted a son," writes Richard. "Richard Oral was the fulfillment of that dream." Born with a lung defect, the infant lived for just 36 hours.

Oral led the family in prayer before the funeral. They huddled together in the green room of ORU's Christ Chapel, backstage at a funeral.

After Richard Oral, Lindsay gave birth to three daughters.

———————

Not long after his daughter and son-in-law died in a tragic plane crash, Oral had a vision of a 900-foot Jesus who told him to build a Christian medical center. This led Oral to build the City of Faith, a $250-million medical center that opened in 1981. Three sparkling gold towers arose on the south side of ORU's campus: a 294-bed hospital, a 60-story clinic, and a 20-story research facility.

The problem was that Tulsa already had more than enough hospital beds. Oral predicted—wrongly, it turned out—that believers would flock to Tulsa for a hybrid of modern medicine and faith healing. Instead, City of Faith hemorrhaged cash.

Around the same time, Oral decided that he needed a Beverly Hills home. ("The old idea that religious people should be poor is nonsense," Oral once said in a TV broadcast.) According to Harry McNevin, the former regent, Oral diverted another $7 million from ORU's endowment: $2.4 million to buy the house (as reported by the *Tulsa Tribune*) and the rest on renovations. "The entire ordeal was kept very quiet," remembers Carlton Pearson, who was a regent at the time. McNevin says he couldn't even get any of the other regents to tell him the address of the house. He resigned from the board.

Strapped for cash, in 1986 ORU shuttered both the dentistry and the law school. (Michele Bachmann graduated from ORU's law school the year it closed.) Things reached a new low in 1987. Oral claimed he had raised the dead. Richard backed him up, recalling a boyhood memory of Oral resurrecting an infant who'd died "right in the middle of my dad's sermon."

To great national ridicule, Oral announced that God had told him he'd be "called home" if he didn't raise $8 million for medical school scholarships. "Let's not let this be my dad's last birthday!" Richard wrote in a fundraising letter.

Ultimately, a dog-track owner in Florida cut a check for the last $1.3 million, and Oral was not called home. But, regardless, the medical center closed in 1989. Then, the rest of City of Faith closed in 1991. ORU's unpaid bills were piling higher and higher.

Oral was growing old. He became even more fixated on his problem of succession, worrying whether or not "Richard could carry it," says Pearson. Sure, Oral racked up debts, but he could also bring in the big money. Richard hadn't proved he could raise funds.

Oral turned to his board of regents for reassurance. "What do you think about Richard? How do you think Richard did last night? What do you think about the future? Do you think he can handle this?" Oral asked the mega-pastors. Pearson remembers, "I kept saying we'll be there for him. Billy Joe [Daugherty], myself, Larry Lea—anybody. Kenneth Copeland, all the preachers on the board. Because all those preachers understood they would want their son to succeed them."

There was a time when Oral planned to divvy up responsibilities, Pearson says: Richard would lead the ministry, and Roberta, a graduate of ORU's law school, would lead the university. Oral told Pearson and Billy Joe Daugherty, "I want you to buttress both of them at either end to support them." That idea was quickly scrapped, says Pearson. "Richard wanted everything."

Passing the scepter in 1993, Oral told his son, "You're anointed by God, chosen by the Lord to be the second president." Oral was leaving ORU about $50 million in debt.

"I'm just delighted that the medal is on you and now off of me," Oral said and promptly retired to his condo on a golf course in Newport Beach, California.

———————

All Souls Unitarian Church is not far from Oral Roberts University. From the pulpit, All Souls' minister dubbed ORU "Babylon on the Arkansas." According to the Book of Daniel, King Belshazzar of Babylon declared that his walled city upon the Euphrates would never fall, all the while feasting and drinking from golden goblets plundered by his father.

All Souls was where Ronnie, Oral and Evelyn's eldest son, attended church with his wife and two adopted kids in the 1970s. Ronnie—Oral's would-be successor, the original beloved son—could not have been more different from his brother. Richard conformed; Ronnie rebelled. Marvin Shirley, a close friend from All Souls, remembers Ronnie as a liberal rationalist who read widely, was fluent in five languages, and viewed the Bible as a historical document. This was the ultimate apostasy for a child of Oral Roberts.

Ronnie was loath to participate in the public performance of being a Roberts, remembers All Souls' minister Dr. John Wolf. "He really wanted nothing to do with it at all out there [at ORU]," says Wolf. Only Evelyn could talk Ronnie into joining the family on Oral's television specials. Oral would demand that Ronnie shave his beard, for a beard stood for hippies and secularism and everything that the ministry was not; Ronnie would refuse. In the programs Ronnie usually ended up in the background or off to the side of the frame somewhere. "It wasn't just a beard. I mean, it was a *beard*," Wolf says, laughing. "He looked like Rasputin for a while."

One Sunday, the televangelist himself showed up at All Souls, Wolf remembers. Oral and Wolf were friendly antagonists in those days. Seeing Ronnie's father in the Unitarian pews, incredulous, Wolf asked, "Oral, what are you doing here?" Oral replied, "Well, I just want to find out what kind of place my kid was going to."

Ronnie eschewed his royal lineage, seeing it as something of an embarrassment. He left town for college and headed to Stanford, dropped out after a year, and joined the army as a linguist, teaching Mandarin in Vietnam. He had himself removed from the family trust fund. After spending three years in a PhD program at the University of Southern California, it was a job offer that brought Ronnie back to Tulsa. He taught at a local high school and started an antiques business. "He despised what his father did," says Shirley, "the way he bilked the poor." According to Shirley, Ronnie had rejected faith healing since adolescence and thought Oral "was in it for the money."

Toward the end of his life, Ronnie developed an addiction to cold medication. Finally, he reached a breaking point. He pleaded guilty to forging a prescription for Tussionex and was placed on probation. A report filed by probation and parole officers noted Ronnie's "strongest feelings about his childhood were those of alienation and rejection from the family because he chose not to adhere to the religious beliefs of his parents and rest of the family."

On Mother's Day of 1982, Evelyn went to visit her eldest son, writes biographer David Edwin Harrell Jr. Ronnie was considering a job that Oral had recently offered him at the university—a move Oral had made many times, always on condition that he shave his beard and quit smoking. Submit, obey. At the time, Ronnie was estranged from his wife and children, living in an apartment just off Peoria Avenue. He had withdrawn from his friends, most of whom hadn't seen him in months. Ronnie always rejected Oral's job offers. Even though he was at the end of the line—his antiques business had failed, his marriage had failed—this time was no different. Ronnie told his mother that he could never take something simply because he was a Roberts.

Exactly one month later, Ronnie's body was found in his car about five miles outside of Tulsa. He'd shot himself in the heart with a .25-caliber gun.

After hearing word from the police, Richard and one of Oral's aides went to Ronnie's apartment, where they found a note. Ronnie had written that he looked forward to seeing his older sister, Rebecca, again. Richard broke the news to Oral and Evelyn.

The Roberts family arranged to have the funeral at ORU, in Christ's Chapel. Oral's eulogy remembered Ronnie "as a man who was never quite the same after a tour of duty during Vietnam." Evelyn believed the devil was to blame for Ronnie's suicide. Roberta, the youngest Roberts child, traced Ronnie's demise to his undergraduate years at Stanford, where everything "his world rested upon" was challenged.

In the aftermath, Oral and Evelyn pored over their memories, wondering if there was something they could have done differently. Richard assured them there wasn't. "I've had to work hard on my dad and mother," Richard told Harrell, the biographer. "It's natural that they would say, 'If I had just done this or that.' It's not true."

"My son had a will of his own," Oral eventually concluded. "My will cannot cancel out anybody's will."

Lives, especially ones that end in suicide, do not lend themselves to neat lines of causation. Even now, over 30 years later, longtime friend Marvin Shirley is still mystified that Ronnie—a sensitive soul, a flautist—would ever shoot a gun, for any reason.

Upon Oral's death in 2009, Bruce Nickerson, a classmate of Ronnie's at Stanford, wrote a eulogy for father and son:

> Ron was gay—a fact that his father could not accept. However Ron told me his father loved him and had never withdrawn support, either financially or emotionally. He just couldn't get beyond Leviticus...

> His family has denied that sexual orientation was a factor [in his suicide]. Remembering his anguish at Stanford, I am certain it was the cause, and that drugs were a futile attempt to mask the pain he must have suffered every day. When I met him he was a terribly troubled youth, struggling with who he was.

It was a time when getting married was the only way to have a normal life, to have a family. "Ronnie was trying very hard to be [part of] the outward couple that Oral wanted," says Wayne Robinson, the former aide.

Oral's youngest child, Roberta, has two adult sons, Randy and Steve. Both are gay. They too were once princelings, living in the royal Roberts compound. In 2005, when Evelyn died, they went together to the funeral. At the grave, they tried to enter the Roberts family tent but were turned away by a guard.

"That's my grandmother inside the coffin," Randy said.

"I know who you are," the guard replied.

The two brothers stood outside the family tent and watched.

Lindsay changed over the years. By the time she was the first lady of ORU, she had a small village of people she could phone who would do her bidding. Sometimes she was sweet and maternal, sometimes cruel and wrathful. She would throw explosive temper tantrums, according to former employees. (Richard and Lindsay did not respond to several interview requests.)

Richard and Lindsay's eldest daughter began attending ORU in the fall of 2003. (All three eventually enrolled.) Whatever the Roberts daughters wished, they received. They wanted a Pilates class to fulfill their PE requirement, so the school had to invent a Pilates class, recalls a faculty member.

"The girls would do things like check out equipment and basically wreck it," says the faculty member. "They seemed to feel like they could get by with most anything."

Professors got in trouble if the Roberts daughters complained about their teaching, says the faculty member, and Richard and Lindsay routinely asked professors to change their daughters' grades.

A charming figure on campus, Richard was popular with the student body. But the alumni had given up on him long ago. Alums had so little confidence in him that only about six percent were ponying up donations.

"The alumni for years wanted somebody to truthfully tell them, 'Here's where the money goes,'" says then-Provost Mark Lewandowski. "There was a lack of open disclosure and true transparency." That's a nice way to say that alums were tired of donating money, only to have it disappear into thin air. Like the nearly $9 million Richard fundraised to build a new student center that never materialized.

Things came to a head on Wednesday, November 14, 2007, a month after Richard and Lindsay's *Larry King* appearance. Oral summoned the tenured faculty for a three-hour meeting. He said he was there to listen, asking them to speak freely and openly. And yet he'd brought Richard along. One by one, speaking directly to Richard, the professors rattled off their complaints.

"You are my friend and my brother in Christ, but it is time for you to go," Provost Mark Lewandowski told Richard. "I cannot continue to serve under you." It was a major act of defiance, coming from Lewandowski, an ORU loyalist and the son of two ORU professors.

Richard pleaded with them to stay, at least for a few more years. He explained his ministry would be under a cloud if he were to be ousted, remembers the faculty member. Lindsay had resigned from the board of regents and, he promised, would no longer involve herself in university affairs.

"My house has been out of order," Richard confessed, according to the faculty member.

Oral doubled down: If Richard left, he'd walk away with him—arm in arm with his anointed son. Oral called on the faculty to forgive Richard, to take a "fresh start." He was 89-years-old at this point. His hearing was going, and he needed a walker. But ever the benevolent dictator, Oral demanded obedience. He asked everyone who agreed with him to stand—an old power play from his repertoire. One professor stood and bravely ventured, "I don't know what you mean by 'fresh start.' I can forgive Richard. But I am not going to allow him to come back as president."

One by one, Oral started grilling the few professors who remained seated. Suddenly, he stopped.

"No, I shouldn't do this. I'm sorry," he said, dropping his head in his big, wrinkled hands.

Richard and Roberta, the two youngest Roberts children, are the only surviving siblings of the four. They weren't exactly on speaking terms in 2009 when it came time for Oral's "homecoming," as he called it, but they headed to the hospital together. Approaching his room, Roberta and Richard heard Oral singing from his hospital bed. He was making his way down the list of hits from his old television shows: "God Is a Good God," "Something Good Is Going to Happen to You," "Expect a Miracle." The two siblings joined in. Richard knew all the words, of course. Those were the tracks off his 1968 debut album, *My Father's Favorite Songs*. Roberta mixed up some of the verses, and Oral, on his deathbed with pneumonia, cut in to correct her—multiple times.

In an interview with KTUL, Richard said that Mart Green, the Hobby Lobby heir who bailed out ORU, "asked me not to come back on campus" after his 2007 ouster. The next time he set foot on ORU's campus was for his father's funeral on December 21, 2009. Richard and Roberta both delivered eulogies. Roberta was terrified of speaking before the crowd in the Mabee Center, the school's main arena. ("I was about to throw up.") Richard—it has to be said—looked a little pleased to be back on stage. He even got to sing a song.

All of the luminaries of the Pentecostal world came to mark the death of the patriarch. Hardly any of them were invited to Oral's graveside service. Richard was meting out punishment for disloyalty—for not standing by him unconditionally as ORU president, says a former regent.

"That was his first chance to be absolutely in charge again," says the regent, "with no one but him calling the shots and commanding the stage since his shameful demotion."

For one day and one day only, Richard ruled supreme.

Roberta was a lonely child. Left with family friends when Oral and Evelyn were off traveling the world, she found companionship in Jesus and became the strictest Pentecostal in the family. Richard and Oral, meanwhile, were golf buddies.

Roberta and Richard have always been at odds. "When we were little, we'd get our allowance and his would be spent within half an hour," Roberta remembers. She was the kind of careful child who saved and budgeted. Richard would come to her, wanting to borrow her allowance. She'd comply. "You think I ever got paid back? No!" she says, with mock exasperation. "That's the story of his life."

As adults, even when both siblings and their families lived in the compound, the two pretty much only saw one another at holidays, remembers Roberta's son Randy. These days, their contact is even more limited. Roberta sent Richard flowers one Easter; the following December, he dropped a birthday card off at her house, leaving the bright pink envelope for her to find in a flowerpot.

On the day Roberta shows me around ORU's campus, she seems nervous and has brought a typed list of stories she wants to tell. It is in many ways a list of firsts: the first time her father took the family to see the empty farmland where he planned to build a university; the dorm where she first lived as an ORU student; the first time she saw the man she would marry ("Almost exactly 42 years ago!"). "First kiss" is number nine on the list.

"Isn't that the neatest?" Roberta asks, pointing out each attraction. Her voice is chipper, but she is clearly pained. Her thin, pink lips are drawn tight. She walks much too quickly, which is not an easy thing to do in heels. A slim woman in her 60s with white hair in a pixie cut, Roberta wears a navy ankle-length polka-dot dress with padded shoulders.

"Dad did not really function as a father, at least not toward me—actually until perhaps a year or so before his passing," she writes in her memoir, *My Dad, Oral Roberts*. Before that, she'd been on the outs with Oral for nearly two decades. It was only after the patriarch's death that Roberta became an ORU trustee.

When we enter Christ's Chapel, a soaring sanctuary filled with light, a calm comes over Roberta. She surveys the stage and the roving TV camera boom. She admires the parquet floors, the plush of the seats. Roberta is unabashed in her love, filled with the wonder of her father's creation.

Roberta faces the writing along the back wall. "'Raise up your students to hear my voice. To go where my light is dim,'" she reads aloud. Smiling, she turns her back to the inscription and begins to recite from memory. "'Their work will exceed yours, and in this I am well pleased,'" she says. "That's what Dad heard from God."

Later, we wander the halls of the Mabee Center, a rotund, flat-topped building trimmed with gold. An elderly security guard pushes aside his lunch when Roberta asks if he'd mind letting us into the television studios.

"Mrs. Potts," says the guard, "you can get into anything you want."

She laughs. "You shouldn't give me anything I wanted, because I might ask for something I shouldn't."

"I doubt that very seriously. I knew your momma too well," the guard replies. "You had two of the nicest young boys," he adds suddenly. "They always said, 'We're the Potts boys. Can we go into the basketball game? We're Potts children, can we please use the phone?'"

"I trained them well," she says.

We enter the cavernous television studio. The lights are off. We stand in silence, looking into the darkness.

Heading back into the sunshine, Roberta calls out to the guard, "Thank you for your kind comments about my sons. Some day they're going to come back to the Lord." A cure for what she calls their "lifestyle"—that's the miracle she's expecting.

"How can I say that there were no excesses, when there were?" Roberta writes of Richard's tenure as ORU president. She says she never learned what exactly was true among the allegations against Richard.

"Did you ever learn specifically that any of them were false? Or blown out of proportion?" I ask. "Um, I guess not. I can't think of anything," she stammers. She pushes all that out of her mind.

As it turns out, donors to Oral Roberts Evangelistic Association do, too. In 2010, the ministry's revenue was nearly $13 million, and Richard and Lindsay paid themselves a combined salary of over $800,000, according to tax filings.

In 2010, the ministry also filed an amended tax return for 2006, saying an internal review of "travel and other expenses" found that $100,602 had been incorrectly billed to the ministry—when really it should've been taxed as executive compensation. In other words, it seemed Richard and Lindsay had put their leisure pursuits on the ministry's tab.

"Dear friend," Richard wrote in a recent letter to potential donors. Out of work? In debt? "Perhaps you feel like you can't sow anything anywhere because your financial situation isn't good right now." Yet, Richard continued, "Nothing could be further from the truth."

Meanwhile, ORU had a succession of presidents outside the Roberts family: A protégé of Oral's, Billy Joe Daugherty, stepped in briefly. Daugherty, the founder of a 17,000-person mega-church across the street from ORU, is said to be the son Oral wished he'd had.[2] Then there was Mark Rutland, followed by the current president, William Wilson.

Having bailed out ORU, the Oklahoma City-based Green family mostly stayed out of the spotlight. Soft-spoken, bespectacled Mart Green, successor to Hobby Lobby CEO David Green (net worth: $5.2

---

2 In the years leading up to the patriarch's death, Carlton Pearson, Oral's "black son," fell from grace in the Pentecostal world after he stopped believing in hell. Carlton and Oral eventually reconciled—albeit on a personal level, not theologically. Pearson's biopic *Come Sunday* is in the works, and Robert Redford is in talks to play Oral in the film.

billion), served as chairman of ORU's board. The Green's donations to ORU now total over $200 million, according to Roberta Roberts Potts.

ORU is finally out of debt. The professors' wrongful termination lawsuits were settled out of court long ago.[3] It is Hobby Lobby—not ORU—making national headlines these days: In June, the Supreme Court ruled in Hobby Lobby's favor, granting a religious exemption to the Affordable Care Act's employer mandate for covering birth control.

––––––––––

Richard's toppling from the ORU throne was not the most noble of exits. And yet, afterward, he seemed relieved, like a burden was lifted, says former Oral Roberts Ministries employee Ryan Rhoades. Facial hair was forbidden under the university's strict anti-hippie dress code. But after Richard and his ministry were expelled from campus, the staff relaxed and grew out beards. Even Richard. Settling into their new offices across town, Richard introduced a four-day workweek. He joked around, carefree at last.

Roberta sometimes catches her brother and sister-in-law on *The Place for Miracles*, Richard and Lindsay's daily half-hour television pro-

––––––––––––––––––––––––––––––––––––––

3 Much was made of Lindsay's alleged relationships with unnamed "under-age males" when the lawsuits hit ORU in 2007. In the years since, Matt Schwoegler, the one-time boyfriend of the youngest Roberts daughter, acknowledged that most of the allegations probably referred to him: the hundreds of late night text messages Lindsay sent teen boys; the nine nights Lindsay and a boy spent in the compound's guest house; the times Lindsay installed a teen boy in her home, leading the Roberts daughters to put deadbolts on their bedroom doors. (Schwoegler has since racked up several criminal convictions, including credit card fraud, forgery, evading arrest, and possession of burglary tools.) Lindsay maintained she "never, ever engaged in any sexual behavior with any man outside of my marriage as the accusations imply." Through the Roberts' attorney, Schwoegler released statements attesting Lindsay had served as a "second mother" and "best friend" to the teen.
   "Do I think she slept with him? No, I don't," says a relative. "Do I think he replaced Richard Oral? In many wrong ways for her, yeah." Lindsay couldn't save her own son, long-ago deceased in infancy, but perhaps she found another lost cause and wanted a second chance.

gram. Oral looms large on the show—my dad this, and your dad that. Richard sings, as always, although his voice is getting a little flat with age.

In late January 2012, an Oklahoma highway patrolman clocked Richard's black Mercedes going 93 miles per hour along the Creek Turnpike, a tollway just south of ORU. A blast of alcohol fumes greeted the highway patrolman when he leaned into the car. Richard failed the first sobriety test, then a second. Richard's DUI mugshot showed an old man wearing a pink shirt and a black jacket, his face bloated and splotchy, his hair white and thinning. It was shortly after midnight of what would have been Oral's 94th birthday.

Later that year, Richard and Lindsay's house, a cobbled mansion in a gated community a few miles south of ORU, went up for sale for $2.15 million. Soon, there were reports that Richard and Lindsay had decamped for Oral's condo in Newport Beach. In December 2013, the building in Tulsa where Richard taped his TV show went up for sale. The show goes on—but broadcasting, it seems, from California. Richard still travels a bit, speaking and holding "miracle healing services" at churches and hotels around the country and, occasionally, overseas. Sometimes, his daughters join him on stage.

In Richard's absence, ORU finally built the student center he had long promised but failed to deliver. It was ORU's first new building in over 30 years. Designed in a nondescript institutional style, nothing is gold about it. Plans are underway to refurbish the ORU-owned CitiPlex Towers (formerly the City of Faith), swapping the gold-tinted windows for blue. The gilded age is over. The time of Technicolor dreams has given way to more modest aspirations: to be, simply, a normal Christian school.

As this past school year came to a close, Mart Green announced the day had come for him to step down as chairman of ORU's board. He'll stay on as a trustee. The school thanked him with a statue in his honor.

The main entrance to ORU is named Billy Joe Daugherty Drive. It is a stately roundabout, lined with the flags of the world. The iconic bronze, 60-foot-tall Praying Hands sculpture sits in the middle—Oral's healing touch immortalized. There is no Richard Roberts Road, or much of anything else to indicate he was ever there at all.

FOUR

OKLAHOMANS AT 100

FATHER OF FIGHT CLUB

The enduring influence of Ralph Ellison's 'Invisible Man.'

By *Michael Mason*

IN 1945, an unassuming black man from Oklahoma City began constructing an intricate book inside a barn in Vermont. Owing to its complexity and sophistication, the book took more than six years to assemble. When Ralph Ellison's *Invisible Man* exploded onto the scene in 1952, it caught countless minds on fire. Critics hailed it as one of the most important books of the times, a masterpiece that confronted America's race problem through a series of blistering allegories. What critics couldn't predict, however, was how prescient and influential the book would become.

The naked woman gyrates sensuously before the group of young black men, conjuring up as much awkwardness as arousal. Moments later, the young men are blindfolded, corralled into a boxing ring, and told to start fighting—a "battle royal." They pummel each other in a chaotic frenzy until one of them is declared victor. Following the fight, the sweaty and bruised contestants all clamor onto a pile of prize money that's rigged with an electrical current, shocking the young men into convulsions. It's all fun and games for the rich white men watching. The finale comes when one of the fighters, "the smartest boy we got out there in Greenwood," stands to deliver a speech. Blood spews from his mouth as he argues for the social responsibility of Negroes.

The opening chapter of Ralph Ellison's *Invisible Man* hooked America in the eye when it first appeared in 1952. It wasn't a friendly book then, and it's grown even more ferocious through the years. In those days, America's civil rights discussions had long been dominated by decades of polite, deferential rhetoric from black leaders like Booker T. Washington. America had never heard from a black man who dared scream in its face, at least not in the way that Ellison did. *Invisible Man* earned him a National Book Award and a reputation.

Ellison was a terror. Young black writers raged because he wasn't helpful to them and sometimes even hurt budding careers; he used his literary status to enjoy privileged (mainly white) company; he was "potentially violent, very violent" according to a friend; he unapologetically fucked women he wasn't supposed to, while married to a woman he loved and tormented. We owe him our thanks for not being a nice guy and instead choosing a life of passion and freedom. True to his sense of artistic integrity, Ellison eventually committed the ultimate crime of modern American literature: He refused to let filmmakers turn his book into a movie.

It only took Hollywood 47 years to figure out how to get around Ellison's disapproval. In 1999, it released a cinematic homage: *Fight Club,* based on the 1996 book by Chuck Palahniuk. Both works have nameless narrators. Both narrators live off the grid in desolate urban settings. Both become leaders of anti-establishment organizations (in *Fight Club* it's Project Mayhem, in *Invisible Man*, it's The Brotherhood). Both wrestle with madness vis-à-vis lobotomies, one by shock, the other by bullet. The two books tackle class warfare and culminate in scenes of social upheaval, with *Invisible Man*'s Harlem erupting into a race riot while *Fight Club* ends with exploding buildings.

In one direct parallel, Ellison's narrator gives the elegy for a fallen Brotherhood comrade, during which he repeats the phrase "His name was Tod Clifton" to drum in a sense of individuality. When a Project Mayhem comrade dies in *Fight Club*, the narrator repeats "His name is Robert Paulson" and the phrase echoes among the group.

And then there are instances where *Fight Club*'s narrator argues with *Invisible Man*:

"Be your own father, young man," a man advises Ellison's narrator.

"Maybe we didn't need a father to complete ourselves," says *Fight Club*.

Nobody can accuse Palahniuk of plagiarizing *Invisible Man*. Palahniuk's book is one continuous monologue, a voice that epitomizes the barbaric yelp of today's disenfranchised cubicle workers. *Fight Club*'s young man tries to reclaim his masculinity while embracing the madness of a world. He's confused, irreverent, caustic, and earnest. Ellison's narrator is older, tougher, and more soulful than Palahniuk's speaker. Readers of *Invisible Man* aren't talked at. Instead, they're led on an allegorical journey through America's racial divide.

While the congruence between *Invisible Man* and *Fight Club* seems uncanny, Chuck Palahniuk claimed that he was actually writing "*The Great Gatsby*, just updated a little." Ellison, on the other hand, credited the modernist poet T.S. Eliot as one of his major inspirations, and Ellison used the influence to let his subconscious flower. *Invisible Man* contains sudden turns into jazz song and poetry, interruptions that confound and entice. Ellison's narrator grapples with his plural identities of student, worker, leader, lover, and citizen, fragmenting his sense of self. *Invisible Man* isn't just a novel, but Ellison's own experience of individuation—the process whereby a person integrates his subconscious into his consciousness and emerges as a more authentic and fully-realized human.[1] As a human experience catalogued, *Invisible Man* is a thank-you note to the monsters who've betrayed you, a fist in the face of power, a triumphant reckoning with the mess in the mirror. Where

---

1 Decades before *Invisible Man*, the psychologist who came up with the theory of individuation wrote the book *Liber Novus*. Carl Jung claimed The Red Book (as it's commonly called) formed the basis for all of his future work on the collective unconscious, synchronicity, and individuation. It remained relatively unknown until it was published in 2009. Illustrated and calligraphed by Jung himself, the book looks like an ancient medieval text, decorated by mythic drawings. The prose reads like a dense sacred text, at times dreamlike and profound and at others inaccessible and unsettling.

Fight Club peaks as a manifesto against corporatism, *Invisible Man* is a transcendent bildungsroman for modern man.

Sixty some years after its publication, *Invisible Man* still feels dangerous and alive. Eyeballs pop out of heads, rape fantasies are entertained, boilers explode. You can practically feel the book ticking in your hands as you turn the pages. *Invisible Man* has a thrilling narrative, but it's also buttressed by existential meditations that now seem prescient. Ellison's notion of invisibility is no longer exclusive to the experience of black Americans, it's become a fundamental trait of the American anti-hero.

When *Fight Club* premiered as a movie, it achieved modest success and, like the book, missed out on major awards. Nevertheless, it became pop-culture shorthand for anything having to do with alienation and social rebellion. Though *Invisible Man* was critically acclaimed, it has never been made into a movie. There are, however, indications that the Ellison estate is softening its no-film stance. In 2013, the estate allowed a stage production of *Invisible Man*, on the condition that the producer kept a strict adherence to the text. The play was well-received but short lived.

At some point, the book will become public domain and a film will be made, Ellison be damned. Whether or not it's a good idea to turn the book into a film is beside the point. *Fight Club* makes its clear that *Invisible Man* has, like any good rebel, already outgrown the control of its creator.

STORIES CARVED IN STONE

A portrait of sculptor Allan Houser on the centennial
anniversary of his birth.

BY *Christina Burke*

PAINTER, ILLUSTRATOR, SCULPTOR, husband, father, innovator,
teacher: Oklahoman Allan Houser was all of these things and more.
Above all else, he was a storyteller.

Throughout a prolific and illustrious career that spanned seven
decades, Houser used paintbrushes, pens, chisels, mallets, and even
jackhammers to bring to life stories of traditional Native culture and
evoke timeless universal emotions. He was known for his energy and experimentation, as well as his entrepreneurship and work ethic, values he
instilled in his children and his students. He demonstrated his versatility
through his adeptness at creating beautifully rendered figures, as well
as elegantly minimal abstracts. Although known for his monumental
sculptures in stone and bronze, he began his career as a painter, and
spent more than 30 years teaching. And he was always drawing, sketch-
ing ideas for his next work no matter the medium or subject matter. His
life and career were auspicious for many reasons, and even 20 years
after his death, he remains one of the best-known and most influential
Native artists of the 20th century; his work is in public and private collections throughout Oklahoma and around the world. This year, with
the centennial of his birth, his home state of Oklahoma celebrates his
many contributions to American art, life, and culture.

Allan Capron Houser (1914 – 1994) was the first Chiricahua Apache child born to the tribe following their release from more than 20 years in captivity as prisoners of war of the U.S. government. His community had been led by such renowned chiefs as Cochise, Victorio, and Mangas Coloradas (Houser's ancestor), and later by the infamous Geronimo. Throughout the 19th century, these powerful leaders and fierce warriors resisted increasing encroachment by non-Indians into traditional Apache territory in the American Southwest (present-day Arizona and New Mexico). Following the four-decades-long "Apache Wars," Native warriors and their families were rounded up and imprisoned first in Florida, later in Alabama, and eventually in Fort Sill in southwestern Oklahoma. It was here that Allan was born to Sam and Blossom Haozous on June 29, 1914. (The spelling of the Apache surname is "Haozous," but early in his life, Allan changed it to the more Anglicized "Houser," which was easier for non-Indians to spell and pronounce.)

Houser was raised on his family's farm near Fort Sill, where he helped tend livestock and harvest fruit trees, corn, cotton, oats, and wheat. He listened to his father's stories of the past, from historical events and battles to traditional ceremonies and ways of life. These stories and his own experiences with Apache culture became the subject of much of his art. With paint and wood and stone and metal, he created images of Apache people engaged in such daily activities as hunting, or sacred rituals like the girls' coming-of-age (Sunrise) ceremonies or the burial rites for a loved one who had died. Many times he illustrated the most basic human group, the family or just mother and child. While such images may appear to be distinctively Apache and feature traditional clothing, they also depict one of the few true universals in life: we all have families.

As a child, Houser was known for his athleticism and his interest in drawing. While the former had a place in farm life, the latter did not. It was not until 1934 when Houser was 20 years old that he had the opportunity to actively pursue his passion for art by making a life-changing move to Santa Fe. It was the capital of New Mexico where Houser's education and career really began, and it would be where he made his most indelible mark on the Native art world through his art and his teaching.

The timing of his move could not have been more fortuitous; Houser's career began at the dawn of contemporary Native fine art in the 20th century. He moved to The Land of Enchantment not for leisure, but to enroll in the recently established "Studio" art program at the Santa Fe Indian School (SFIS). The program was created in 1932 by Dorothy Dunn, a teacher trained at the Art Institute of Chicago who had already taught Native students at schools in two Pueblo communities in New Mexico. This was a time of great change in federal Indian policy, as those in government sought to address the devastation of the Great Depression in Native communities. Among the policy changes were a lifting of the ban on teaching traditionally Native arts in Bureau of Indian Affairs (BIA) schools like that in Santa Fe, and the establishment in 1934 of the Indian Arts and Crafts Board (IACB). Both of these were seen as ways to encourage Native people to develop economic sustainability through the creation and sale of art. Some Native artists, including Allan Houser, were even part of Works Progress Administration (WPA) projects, and commissioned to paint murals in government buildings in Washington, D.C., and throughout the country.

———————

At about the same time, Oscar Jacobson, a professor of art at the University of Oklahoma in Norman, had taken on a group of students known as the Kiowa Six. These painters (Spencer Asah, James Auchiah, Jack Hokeah, Stephen Mopope, Lois Smoky, and Monroe Tsatoke) are credited as among the first Native people to pursue formal art education at the university level. In addition, their work was displayed as fine art in exhibitions in the U.S. and Europe, and was published in a portfolio that remains one of the most important publications of Native art to this day.

Houser began his art education in the midst of this revitalization of Native art, and in Santa Fe no less, which was already recognized as the heart of the Native art world. It has long been a nexus for trade and commerce among Native peoples (Pueblo, Navajo, Apache, and others) and between Native and non-Native peoples, particularly the Spanish and Anglo (American). In 1922, it became the site of the Santa Fe Indian Market, now the oldest and most prestigious competitive show of Native art. Forty years later, it became the home of the Institute of American Indian Arts, a unique academic institution exclusively for Native students, and where Houser taught for many years.

Dorothy Dunn's "Studio" program was long-lived and had an incredible impact on Native painting. Her method of teaching was based on her belief that students should paint what they know from their particular tribes and communities, and that they should portray such scenes in a "traditional" manner. By this she meant a flat style of painting that did not include background, foreground, perspective, or shading (some of the hallmarks of established Western art practice). Appropriate subject matter was deemed to be scenes of supposed Native life, such as hunting, warfare, and ceremonies.

This perspective was based on a commonly held idea that Native peoples and their cultures were vanishing because of the assimilation into mainstream American culture and the incredible pressures imposed by government policies, Christian missionaries, a capitalist economic system, and formal schooling where Native languages and ways were forbidden. With a sense of reform and reclamation, Dunn encouraged her students to preserve such traditions by painting them in a rigid style that she deemed appropriate. Although Houser did create many works in this flat style, he bristled under such unyielding and ill-informed ideas about who Native people were and how they lived.

Houser painted figurative work and often portrayed Apache people engaged in traditional activities and rituals, but he also longed for more—more instruction on Western painting techniques and styles, and more freedom to explore other non-Native subjects. He was always a voracious reader and so continued his pursuit of knowledge outside the classroom, devouring books on such Western artists and illustrators such as Frederic Remington, whose sensitive depictions of animals, especially horses, was always an inspiration to Houser. Throughout his career, he was inspired and guided by his identity as an Apache and his knowledge of history and culture, as well as his confidence in experimenting with new ways of doing things.

His move to Santa Fe was a catalyst for many important events in his life and career. In 1937, while still a student at the SFIS, Houser had his first solo exhibition of work at the Museum of New Mexico in Santa Fe. In 1938 and '39, he and classmate Gerald Nailor (Navajo, 1917–1952) were commissioned to paint murals for the Department of the Interior in Washington, D.C. He had a watershed year in 1939 when he married Anna Marie Gallegos (a Navajo woman with whom he had four sons) and had his work shown in three exhibitions across the country, at the Art Institute of Chicago, the New York World's Fair, and at the Golden Gate Exposition in San Francisco. The following year, Houser painted a fresco mural with Norwegian artist Olle Nordmark in his hometown at the Fort Sill Indian School. From 1941 to 1947 he, like many other Americans, worked in variety of war-related jobs, primarily construction projects in Los Angeles. While there, he took advantage of the many museums in the area, learning independently about various European and American artists and their work.

In 1947 he learned of a competition sponsored by the alumni association of Haskell Institute, an Indian school in Lawrence, Kansas. The winning artist would be commissioned to create a sculpture to honor fallen Native veterans. Although Houser had only ever created small wooden carvings and not life-size (much less monumental) sculptures, he decided to enter the competition. His sketch of the larger-than-life *Comrade In Mourning* won the contest, and the resulting seven-foot marble figure was Houser's first real foray into sculpture.

Houser's career really began to take off with this commission, as well as with the awards and accolades he was receiving from museums and art organizations across the country and around the world. For instance, he won a fellowship from the Guggenheim Foundation in 1949 and Les Palmes Academique from the French government in 1954. In 1950 he created a series of unique dioramas for the IACB's Southern Plains Museum in Anadarko, Oklahoma, and, in 1958, was commissioned to design the commemorative medal for the Society of Medalists.

Among the competitions he entered was the Philbrook Indian Annual, a juried exhibition primarily for painters and sculptors. The Annual ran from 1946 through 1979, and Houser was active as both a participant (entering 22 paintings and 9 sculptures) and a judge. He won a record of five Grand Awards, tying with his contemporary Oscar Howe (Yanktonai, 1915 – 1983) for the most of these coveted Best of Shows. His first Grand Award was for a watercolor called *Apache Baby Burial* (1948), which depicts a family mourning the loss of a young child.

One might ask why an artist, any artist, would choose to illustrate such a scene. Although the image is of traditional Apache burial rites, the emotions of all the family members in the painting are universal; any family that has endured such a tragedy can relate to the pain and grief of this type of tragedy.

The last Grand Award he won, 20 years later, was for an ebony carving titled *Sacred Rain Arrow,* which in 1968 became the first sculpture to win this award. In this sleek, stylized sculpture we do not see an entire figure, but only the man's left arm, head, and right hand. The bow and arrow are merely hinted at—not fully defined with the wood, but rather left to the imagination with just a suggestion of the form. (The following year he was honored with the Waite Phillips Award for Lifetime Achievement for his many contributions to Native American art.) Twenty years later he created a bronze version with the same title, editions of which can be seen throughout the country, including in front of the Gilcrease Museum of the Americas in Tulsa, Oklahoma. Since 2008, an image of the bronze sculpture has been on the Oklahoma license plate.

Not only was Houser a prolific artist who won honors for his many paintings and sculptures, he was also a dedicated teacher, working with students for nearly 30 years before retiring to focus on his own art in 1975. For more than a decade (1951–1962) he taught painting, sculpture, textiles, and graphic design at the Inter-Mountain Indian School, a vocational school primarily for Navajo students in Brigham, Utah. In keeping with his interest in life-long learning, he not only taught classes, but also took classes, enrolling in extension courses at Utah State College. It was during this time that he also illustrated nine children's books for the *Indian Reader Series,* a collection of Native-themed books for which many Native artists served as illustrators from the 1930s through the 1960s.

———————

By the late 1950s, the Native art world was becoming contentious as many were constricted by the expectations and definitions of what was Native art. The commonly held perspective about "traditional" Indian painting that had been articulated by Dorothy Dunn at the Studio was still affecting what was taught, created, and purchased by both individual and institutional collectors. The question of who was defining Native art came to a head in 1958 when an abstract painting by Oscar Howe titled *Umine Wacipe* (War and Peace Dance) was rejected by judges at the Philbrook Indian Annual for being too contemporary and not authentically "Indian." An outraged Howe wrote a scathing letter to Philbrook protesting that only Native artists can define what authentic Native art is. In response the museum added a new category for "Non-Traditional Painting" the following year.

But this type of stagnation chafing Howe in Oklahoma was being felt by Native artists in the Southwest as well. In response to a growing outcry from Native artists and others, the Rockefeller Foundation sponsored a series of summer workshops at the University of Arizona in Tucson to address the status and future of Native art. Artists like Houser joined in discussions with academics, curators, traders, government agents, and others to discuss ideas about authenticity, culture change, individuality, and modernity, as well as the reality of the market at galleries, museums, shows, and trading posts.

One of the other major points of discussion was that Native art education was unacceptable and needed to be changed drastically. It was in the wake of this cry for change that the Institute of American Indian Arts (IAIA) was founded in Santa Fe in 1962. This unique school was created exclusively for Native students and was staffed primarily by Native instructors. Houser was among the first teachers hired at "The Institute," along with Lloyd Kiva New (Cherokee, 1916 – 2002), Charles Loloma (Hopi, 1921 – 1991), Fritz Scholder (Luiseño, 1937 – 2005), and others. One of the things these artists had in common was motivation to experiment and push boundaries and expectations themselves as individual artists and Native art in general. The Institute created a progressive atmosphere in which these innovators encouraged their students to express themselves through their art, whether painting, sculpture, jewelry, or other media.

———————

Houser taught at IAIA for 13 years before retiring in 1975 to focus exclusively on his own creative process. But his time at the Institute was a productive one during which he flourished, experimenting with carving wood and stone and casting bronze. His first castings were in 1967 at the Nambé Mills Foundry in Pojoaque, New Mexico, near Santa

Fe. By casting, Houser could create multiple pieces in editions, but in the late 1960s and early 1970s he was fabricating sculptures, welding pieces of metal together to create a single, unique piece. And he continued to carve sculptures from stone.

With all of these materials and techniques, he experimented with contrasts, creating a variety of textures, and playing with positive and negative spaces. Many of his stone sculptures feature a contrast between highly polished areas (faces on his figurative pieces) with areas left rough and textured to depict such elements as hair or clothing. On some of his more abstract metal sculptures, there is both the presence and absence of materials, as in the elegantly beautiful *Apache Mask* (1976) in which the upturned face is both there (in bronze) and not there. Such work was the distillation of an image to its very essence of structure.

Later in life, Houser continued to receive recognition and accolades for his work, and not just in the Native art world. In the 1970s he had solo shows at the State Capitol in Santa Fe and at the Hood Museum at Dartmouth College. In 1981, his paintings were included in an exhibition at the Kennedy Center in Washington, D.C., and his sculptures were exhibited at the Salon d'Automne at the Grand Palais in Paris. In 1983, he had exhibitions in both France and Germany, and was honored by the State of Oklahoma with the Governor's Award for Visual Arts. In 1986, he was commissioned to create a bust of Geronimo, to commemorate the 100th anniversary of the surrender of the Chiracahua's (and the beginning of their decades-long incarceration). Copies of the bust are on display at the Fort Sill Apache Tribal Center in Oklahoma and the National Portrait Gallery in Washington, D.C. In 1992, Houser became the first Native person to receive one of the nation's highest honors, the National Medal of Arts, in a ceremony presided over by President George H.W. Bush. The following year, IAIA honored him by establishing the Allan Houser Park on their campus in downtown Santa Fe.

Here in Oklahoma, one can see Houser's work at museums and private collections, as well as throughout the campus of the University of Oklahoma in Norman, and even on the grounds of the State Capitol on Oklahoma City. His images are powerful and have universal appeal in their beauty and in the emotions they depict and evoke. They remind us that we are all human.

TORMENT RELIEVED IN SONG

John Berryman's poetry sprang forth from pain and anguish.

By *Cheryl Pallant*

ON OCTOBER 25, 1914, banker John Allyn Smith and schoolteacher Martha Little welcomed their first of two sons, John Allyn Smith Jr.—now known to the world as John Berryman.

Berryman was born in McAlester, Oklahoma, a town of roughly 17,000 people, about the same size then as it is today, best known for housing prison inmates and a munitions plant. In 2005, Friends of Libraries in Oklahoma added to the city's identity by dedicating McAlester an Oklahoma Literary Landmark in recognition of Berryman, who is the only Oklahoman to win the Pulitzer Prize, the National Book Award, and the Bollingen Prize (among numerous other awards).

On the centennial of his birth, critics are questioning Berryman's fit into the pantheon of poets. How did he contribute to the field? How distinctive is his music? What type of poet was he? What type of man? In reading his books, what can we learn about ourselves?

Forty-two years after his tragic suicide, interest in his work continues through rereleases of previous publications, the arrival of never-before-printed books, and conferences in Minneapolis, Minnesota, and Dublin, Ireland.

We look because he was a poet. Because he read volumes and elevated the mind and its poetic expression above all else. His pain and accomplishments rouse our sympathy, scorn, and admiration.

In 1911, Berryman's father, at age 24, moved from Minnesota to work with his two brothers for a bank in Holdenville, Oklahoma. One brother died soon after of pneumonia, and the other got caught up in a bank scandal and disappeared. Consequently, his father moved to another bank in Sasakwa where, at a boarding house, he met Martha Little, who was seven years younger than him and had recently arrived from Missouri. He allegedly forced himself upon her and later coerced her into marriage at All Saints Catholic Church in McAlester.

Questing for a decent salary to start a family, the newlyweds moved to Lamar, then to Wagoner, and then to Tampa, Florida, to take advantage of the land boom. There they opened a restaurant, but the boom quickly busted and Berryman's father lost all he had gained, monetarily and matrimonially. The restaurant failed, and Martha began an affair with John Angus Berryman. John Allyn Smith, chain-smoking, drinking heavily, and disillusioned by his losses, ended his life with a bullet to his chest, a tragedy that some claim young Berryman witnessed. Several months later, Martha married John Angus Berryman, who adopted her two sons, and changed John Allyn Smith Jr.'s name to John Allyn Berryman.

The loss of his father and a love-hate relationship with his mother would color Berryman's days for the duration of his life. He would suffer from severe mood swings (likely an undiagnosed bipolar condition), and self-medicate with alcohol, women, and writing.

Berryman was sent to boarding school in South Kent, Connecticut, in 1928, where upperclassmen bullied him. He furthered his education at Columbia University, where one of his teachers, Mark Van Doren, a poet, writer, and critic, planted the seed of Berryman becoming a poet. With a modest interest in other subjects, Berryman attended Van Doren's classes with great enthusiasm, their only competition being a goal of bedding as many women as possible.

College established a welcomed and needed focus for Berryman: poetry. He studied Shakespeare and wrote sonnets, and experienced early success when several of his poems appeared in *The Columbia Review* and off-campus publications such as *The Nation*.

Berryman, like many Anglo-centric poets of his time, looked toward Europe—particularly the English and Irish—for their great writers. He spent two years at Clare College in Cambridge, where he reveled in Shakespeare and consumed Yeats and Auden, who influenced his form and technique. Upon the passing of Yeats, whom he considered the "latest, perhaps the last, master of English poetry," Berryman wrote:

> There passed away from eye, from hand,
> The greatest among us. Let the bells toll.
> He alone saw to the core, and having seen
> Terror on all sides, was compassionate.

When Berryman returned from England, he wrote manically, often neglecting to eat or shave or pay rent. His first book, *Poems,* was published in 1942 by New Directions Publishing. Six years later, William Sloane Associates published *The Dispossessed.* Neither book earned him wanted recognition. In reference to the latter book, Randall Jarrell wrote in *The Nation* that Berryman was "a complicated, nervous, and intelligent [poet]" whose poetry "was too derivative of W.B. Yeats."

Berryman's devotion to writing regularly tilted into self-destruction. To fuel his writing, he drank. To celebrate a poem's publication, he drank. To handle the disappointment of rejection, he drank. If his mother refused to read his work, or he felt desolate or suicidal, or met a publisher or a woman, he drank. In the years to come, the drinking escalated into blackouts, delirium tremens, and attempts at detoxing with periodic stays in the hospital. He managed to dry out for a period, but always the spirit of alcohol found a way to ravage him.

His devotion and the rigor of writing also kept him sober and sane. In his poem "Waking Up," Berryman writes about alcohol's hold on him:

> Sober Henry hid his glass
> Henry wd have to be sober fr here out.
> It was bitter cold out
> & bitter cold in...

His voluntary drug makes his brain swim,
he holds things that aren't here,
sees what never was. It's clear...

Berryman taught at Princeton, Harvard, the University of Vermont, Bard College, and the University of Minnesota, among others. He ran after whatever position came available, semester-long or lengthier. He exhibited little patience for idle or mediocre students and unleashed his temper to intimidate students into dropping his classes. Those who stayed, like Philip Levine, a student of his at Iowa University, said that Berryman made "the study of poetry... the center of the world."

Berryman married three times, first to Eileen Simpson (1942–1956), then to Ann Levine (1956–1959), and then to Kate Donahue (1961–1972). Each woman, pivotal to his writing, read and commented on his work. As importantly, they held him together when his own emotional and psychological demons tore him apart. They withstood his drunken bouts, his self-loathing and doubts, his arrogant rants, and his infidelities with both single and married women, often the spouses of colleagues. Of women, Berryman writes:

Filling her compact & delicious body
with chicken paprika, she glanced at me
twice.
Fainting with interest, I hungered back
and only the act of her husband & four other people
kept me from springing on her...

Simpson and Levine ultimately left him. Donahue was on the brink, but his life ended before she drew up the papers.

When Berryman took up the topic of writing about 17th-century Puritan poet Anne Bradstreet, it wasn't so much out of admiration for her work as it was that she represented yet another woman—a poet no less—to possess. He claimed Bradstreet summoned him from her nearly 300-year-old grave, and he obliged. The result was *Homage to Mistress Bradstreet*, originally published in the *Partisan Review* in 1953, then as a book in 1956. The book's 57 lyrical stanzas examine her life and art and garnered substantial praise. The work placed him on par with fellow male poets whom he considered peers and competition. Said Delmore Schwartz about the book, it is "the most distinguished long poem by an American since *The Waste Land*." From *Homage to Mistress Bradstreet*:

> Jaw-ript, rot with its wisdom, rending then;
> then not. When the mouth dies, who misses you?
> Your master never died,
> Simon ah thirty years past you—
> Pockmarkt & westward staring on a haggard deck
> it seems I find you, young. I come to check,
> I come to stay with you,
> and the Governor, & Father, & Simon, & the huddled men.

In *Homage to Mistress Bradstreet*, Berryman steps away from the shadow of Yeats and begins to develop his own voice. The primarily iambic rhythm of his lines breaks from those of his awed predecessor, and a lusty, more American vernacular emerges. The break is essential to establish himself as anything other than a copyist.

Berryman's American vernacular and distinctive style takes firm hold in *77 Dream Songs*, a series of short, 18-line lyrics in three stanzas that earned him a Pulitzer Prize. He then feverishly wrote its sequel, *His Toy, His Dream, His Rest,* which won him the National Book Award and the Bollingen Prize. Both books were published together as *The Dream Songs* in 1969 by Farrar, Straus & Giroux.

Dream Songs, drawn from years of psychoanalysis, a response to Whitman's *Song of Myself,* and a desire to conceive an epic work, is based on a character named Henry—ranter, lamenter, minstrel singer, and an irrepressible voice who permits a range and depth of expression previously unseen in Berryman's writing. As a literary foil for Berryman (though Berrymen denies the connection), Henry, often using broken English and made-up words, gushes on about paternal suicide, addiction to sex and alcohol, and displeasure with the horror of the Vietnam War. Visible is a fragile ego, at times bloated with self-importance, other times desperate for inflating.

Visible, too, are constant shifts in tone, diction, and syntax, a loosening into slang and wordplay. The iambic music is still present but mixed with blues and jazz. He riffs on his earlier reliance on intellectualism and permits a deeper, more personal engagement with language and topic. In "Dream Song 40," he writes:

> I'm scared a lonely. Never see my son,
> easy be not to see anyone,
> combers out to sea
> know they're goin somewhere but not me.
> Got a little poison, got a little gun,
> I'm scared a lonely

The tremendous inspiration and output of these poems—385 in *The Dream Songs*, and many more unpublished—came at a high price. His hospital stays increased in frequency and length; he lost entire days to delirium as the demons of alcohol and depression tightened their grips. Doctors warned that a failure to control his drinking would have fatal consequences. His third wife, Kate Donohue, threatened him with divorce.

The Dream Songs delivered accolades, celebrity, and steady employment. Berryman wrote another collection with Henry, a series of criticism, and a novel. He underwent a religious awakening that is represented in the last book he completed, *Delusions*. Several more books were in the works, but the darkness pursuing him for decades began to close in.

While teaching at University of Minnesota, Berryman walked to the Washington Avenue Bridge over the Mississippi River, climbed onto the railing, waved to passing students, and plummeted to his death.

———————

What makes a good poet? It depends on who does the asking and the context from which they judge. Berryman stated that great poetry springs forth from pain and anguish, a definition that suits him perfectly.

"My idea is this: The artist is extremely lucky who is presented with the worst possible ordeal which will not actually kill him ...Beethoven's deafness, Goya's deafness, Milton's blindness, that kind of thing," Berryman said in a 1970 interview.

Rarely did he praise female writers other than Adrienne Rich and Elizabeth Bishop. Works by writers of color, other than Ralph Ellison, did not appear on his radar. He disdained the work of Allen Ginsberg, describing *Howl* as "public masturbation."

Many have categorized Berryman as a confessional poet, a label he abhorred. He preferred the moniker "middle generation": those belonging to the period between the modernists and the post-modernists.

Berryman viewed poetry from a white male perspective, a sexist and patriarchal myopia largely shared by many of his time, a take on intelligence that left vast segments of the population without voice or consideration. He held a parochial vision and understanding of history and culture, empty, for the most part, of countries outside the U.S. Yet no life of easy, settled privilege awaited him as he might have hoped. The interlopers were many: World War II, his father's suicide, mental illness, the Korean War, the Vietnam War, womanizing, alcohol. All appear in his poetry.

Many poets of his generation such as Randall Jarrell, Hart Crane, Sylvia Plath, and Anne Sexton took their own lives. There's something beguiling or fetishistic about an artist's tragedy, a demise that penetrates the work in one field and bleeds into another. Berryman's death has been the source of lyrics for the Brooklyn band The Hold Steady and for rockers Okkervil River. Berryman makes an appearance in James Franco's *The Broken Tower*, a movie about the ill-fated poet Hart Crane.

Were it not for *The Dream Songs*, Friends of Libraries in Oklahoma likely would not have dedicated the McAlester as an Oklahoma Literary Landmark. It's unlikely, too, that the centennial of his birth would warrant much attention.

In *The Dream Songs*, Berryman let down his metered guard and let language flow elegiacally. In it, we see a search for knowledge and values, a reflection of personal and political tumult, a voice wrestling with violent feelings of love, death, religion, and politics. He captures a difficult yet distinctive music. To read him is to wrestle with poetry and the collision of life with art.

LAFFERTY LOST AND FOUND

A pioneer of Oklahoma sci-fi celebrates 100.

By *Natasha Ball*

THEY CONVENED IN A MEETING ROOM in the back of an old Borden's Cafeteria. A bald man with a soft paunch, looking perfectly at home at the first meeting of Oklahoma Science Fiction Writers, sat wordlessly in the back, peering over thick glasses. His name, R.A. Lafferty—that's Raphael Aloysius, but usually he settled for just Ray—seemed familiar to Warren Brown and the others. He'd seen Lafferty's name in his old copies of *Galaxy*, one of the preeminent magazines of science fiction and fantasy writing. Then there was Lafferty's *Okla Hannali*, a novel about a great Choctaw. Dee Brown, author of *Bury My Heart at Wounded Knee*, called it "art applied to history"; *The Wall Street Journal* said it was "elemental Americana and a great deal of fun." Married there were years of research with folklore, fantasy, and humor; Brown had marveled. He still has the copy he picked up at a JC Penney in Toledo, back when there were still bookstores in JC Penney.

By that time—1977—R.A. Lafferty had written much of what would, by the end of his life, total more than 200 short stories and more than a dozen novels. He had been awarded the Hugo Award, one of the highest prizes in science fiction and fantasy writing, early in his career. Harlan Ellison and Gene Wolfe were lavish in their praise. A fan of languages, Lafferty could read the copies of his novels and short stories that had been translated to French, Italian, German, and Dutch; the ones in Japanese, though, gave him some trouble. He'd been nominated for several more awards, but Lafferty, a writer whose work defied classification and confounded the traditions of the genre, didn't quite fit the bill.

Most of Lafferty's stories begin ordinarily enough. In "Nine Hundred Grandmothers," the short story that carries the name of a collection cherished by the small core of Lafferty fans, a man wonders how life began. Then, in the space of a few hundred words, he discovers a cave filled with beings who never die. "It is a foolish alien custom which we see no reason to imitate," one of them says. In "The Six Fingers of Time," another landmark Lafferty work, a man shatters a glass and an alarm clock before he realizes the cause of his clumsiness: he controls the flow of time, a problematic new reflex. Lafferty claimed G.K. Chesterton and Balzac as influences. "Neither of them could plot worth a dam [sic], and both of them got along without any nonsense about structure or outline," he once wrote.

Throughout his life, Oklahoma, and early Tulsa in particular, was a recurring character in Lafferty's work, at times as itself, at others in clever disguise. There's the short story "In Our Block," when two men tour a deserted dead end a block long, a suggestion of Lafferty's own Trenton Avenue in Tulsa, where he lived quietly and watched the young city unfold for the better part of seven decades. The men stumble upon a mini boomtown that seems to have appeared out of thin air, a row of shanty shops filled with winking, grinning out-of-towners. There they ship 60,000-pound loads out of seven-foot shacks, type letters with their tongues, and wonder at the market for $100 automobiles. Tulsa shows up again in "Grey Ghost: A Reminiscence." Lafferty writes of a (very) close encounter with the dead on Halloween night, 1924, near "the old Electric Park which was south of Tulsa, between the Peoria Road and the Arkansas River. It was a dog-racing track complete with electric rabbit." Andrew Ferguson, a Lafferty scholar who is at work on the writer's biography, puts Lafferty in a new genre: Oklahoma fusion storytelling.

"He was deeply invested in bringing out this oral narrative technique he learned from his father and uncles and his Irish aunts who had been out on the Oklahoma frontier, and other oral storytellers in the South Pacific [during his service] in World War II and Army buddies there, Cherokee and Choctaw storytellers—bringing all these techniques into written and very self-aware fiction on the page," Ferguson said. As a result, "no other author does what he does with language. No one gets away with the things he gets away with."

Brown guessed Lafferty showed up to that first OSFW meeting in search of the next generation of sci-fi readers and writers, some sign of breaking dawn. The tide had turned after Lafferty's early success, Ferguson said. Publishing changed in the '70s and '80s, and science fiction wasn't spared. The New Wave, a fold in the genre where Lafferty's work is most often filed, was defined by the rebellion and experimentation emblematic of the '60s counterculture. It was literary work based on soft rather than hard science. Still, Lafferty's conservative politics and distaste of the gratuitous sex scene put him on the fringe even there.

Ferguson has been looking into how publishing changed during Lafferty's time. By then publishers had early versions of software that showed what sold and what didn't. Cult and niche authors, those whose work was more experimental than it was marketable, were pruned from editors' lists. By the date of the first meeting of OSFW, genre traditions were reasserted, and publishing houses pandered to readers who approached a bookstand like a fast-food menu—fewer choices, no surprises, what you see is what you get. Lafferty couldn't promise to sell tens of thousands of copies of tall tales or campfire stories masquerading as sci-fi, and he couldn't bank on much crossover. "Science-fiction fans don't read historical novels," reads one Lafferty quote.

Galaxy, one of the magazines that originally proliferated Lafferty's work, stopped accepting his submissions after editor Frederik Pohl, who split the 1973 Hugo with Lafferty, left his post. Lafferty was a fixture at science-fiction conferences. He delivered speeches and served on panels, but he became notorious for being always first in line at cocktail hour—stories of Lafferty convincing charitable women to sit on his lap proliferated, echoed by similar flirtations in his correspondence with female friends and fans. Film and video game deals for Lafferty's novels and short stories languished or fell through. His novels and collections of short stories fell out of print or went to garage presses for infinitesimal runs. Even in his hometown, the daily newspapers sent him reporters only a few times every decade. On the same shelves where Lafferty kept his Hugo, silver and rocket-shaped, was his "Invisible Little Man Award," given to him by a science-fiction group in California for work that should be better appreciated.

Still, Lafferty wasn't one to complain. "This is the only job in the world where you can make a fair living by working an hour a day," he told a *Tulsa Tribune* reporter; he wrote elsewhere that he doesn't know why more people don't do it. In spite of his setbacks, he wrote as exuberantly as ever. He became a regular contributor to the OSFW newsletter. He poked fun by writing petty letters to the editor, and he wrote poems for the club's poetry anthology under names like Mary Mystic O'Trassy and Audifax O'Hanlon. He was a lively correspondent, writing long letters to fans that were as vivid and surreal as any of his published work. Later, he included apologies for his arthritic typing in the postscripts.

Lafferty attended most of the OSFW meetings, Brown said. Dozens of times, Brown waited outside the Lafferty house, a shaded brick bungalow where Trenton comes to a T, letting his '78 Nova idle. Lafferty knew Tulsa's streets—some days he would walk for miles, prowling the sidewalks of Cherry Street and Swan Lake—but he wouldn't drive, not to the OSFW meetings or anywhere else. He needed a ride, and Brown lived closest. Lafferty never said much on the commute, Brown said, or at any other time. Always more talkative on the page, he'd greet other OSFW members at the junk-food table, perhaps pat them on the shoulder. Club members would read their new work, and most of the time Lafferty—surely crushing the hopes of the writers—sat silent. Once or twice Brown remembers him saying, "Well, that may not be quite there," or, "Well, I think you can probably sell that." Only once did he offer Brown, whose work was published for the first time during those days of driving Lafferty, something more on an early version of his work: "You are a cold fish. But you could be a hot fish."

Warren Brown might have emerged as a published writer without the self-dubbed "cranky old man from Tulsa," but it's hard to imagine what would have happened to Neil Gaiman. Lafferty was his favorite author in the world, he said. "His stories brimmed with ideas that no one had ever thought before. The use of language was uniquely his own—a Lafferty sentence is instantly utterly recognizable," Gaiman wrote of Lafferty, in an introduction to the story in Martin H. Greenberg's *My Favorite Fantasy Story*. "The cockeyed, strange, and wonderful world he painted in his tales often seems nearer to our own, more joyful and more recognizable than many a more worthy or more literal account by other authors the world stopped to notice."

When he was 19, Gaiman dug Lafferty's address out of the back of a library book and wrote to him, asking for advice on becoming an author. Tulsa, thanks to Lafferty, is for him a place of literary magic. "He told me how to become an author, and his advice was very good advice, and so I did. It left me quite certain that the finest literary advice in the world came from Tulsa, Oklahoma, for it did in my case," Gaiman said. Gaiman wondered on his blog just months before Lafferty died if he would ever be recognized as a genius.

Lafferty left the earth unceremoniously, from a Broken Arrow nursing home in the spring of 2002. The rights to his short stories and more than two dozen novels and dozens of unpublished works were unsettled for nearly a decade. Plans to make a home for Lafferty's literary estate at OSFW fell through, Brown said, so Lafferty's heirs placed a classified ad in *Locus*, a news and trade journal for the science-fiction and fantasy genre. It didn't go unnoticed. Blogs and forums buzzed with rumors and speculation about what would happen to Lafferty's works, who the next custodian would be, and whether or not the stories and novels would be available again.

In 2011, Locus Science Fiction Foundation, the 501(c)3 publisher of the magazine and its website, purchased the Lafferty literary estate. "Neil Gaiman is on our board, and he really wanted to do it," said Liza Groen Trombi, the magazine's editor and president of the board of the LSFF. The hope is that Locus will bring Lafferty's work back into circulation, outside of anthologies and collectors' editions. Meanwhile, Lafferty still earns ink in Japan. Ferguson heard that *Hayakawa's SF Magazine* will feature Lafferty in its November issue in celebration of his centennial. The World Fantasy Convention is planning its own tribute to Lafferty at the 2014 event in Washington, D.C., to take place the weekend of Lafferty's 100th birthday, with a panel hosted by Ferguson. Over the summer Gaiman talked to *The Guardian* for a lengthy profile of Lafferty, helping the publication to bill him as the greatest science-fiction writer you've never heard of. Rumors of interest from studios and filmmakers are swirling. A Lafferty resurgence seems to be at hand. Jim Thompson, the writer behind *The Grifters* and *The Killer Inside Me* who was born in Anadarko while the Lafferty family decided where to settle in Oklahoma, would put his elbow in Lafferty's ribs. He would know what it's like to wait more than a decade in the grave, long after the papers ran the short obits on the pulp-fiction writer next door, before the living realized what they had lost.

Brown got a call after Lafferty's home sold. The new owners had something, and they weren't quite sure what to do with it. Brown had been inside the house, sat in the living room during OSFW meetings, but Lafferty had never invited him or any of the club members into his office. By then it had been cleaned out of its wall-to-wall, floor-to-ceiling bookshelves filled with Shakespeare, dictionaries of foreign languages, horror stories, *Li'l Abner*, and religious texts (Lafferty, a Christ the King parishioner and a Cascia Hall grad, was a devout Roman Catholic and, as a passage in his correspondence states, he "cannot understand how an intelligent person can be anything else").

What was left was the door. Nearly every square inch was covered in a mysterious collage, save for the keyhole and crystal knob. Down the center were clippings of images of fine art, mostly women in portrait; a cacophony of cartoons and children's Valentines framed them. Ancient animals and obsolete farming tools were pasted in a corner together, destined to forever coexist. It was wonderful to see, Brown said. He knew about Lafferty's long walks and suspected he went for his typewriter and carbon paper (he worked for an electrical supply company until he turned to writing full time at age 45, but he preferred the analog) not to write but rather to type; for Brown, the door seemed to confirm it. Ferguson saw it, too. "I'm glad it was salvaged," he said. "I have to imagine it was an emblem of how his mind must have worked, this huge array of kaleidoscopic imagery, all shuffling in and demanding attention all at once… filling every available area. That's certainly what his stories do."

FIVE

JOURNEYS NEAR AND FAR

DISPATCHES FROM
THE WEEDPATCH CAMP

Every year, Okies all over the country trek back to the Arvin
Migrant Center in Southern California for the Dust Bowl Festival.

By *Thomas Conner*

LIKE MANY PEJORATIVES, the word "Okie" has been reclaimed—
particularly within the borders of its namesake state—as a proud regional identifier. Nearly a century ago, however, Californians spat the
term toward the poor migrant families (whether they were actually
from Oklahoma or not) rolling in across the deserts, desperate for food,
shelter, and work.

Now here I am at a festival in southern California, surrounded by
Okies—the real deal—and standing next to me is a fella wearing a dark
blue t-shirt blaring a single word in white capital letters across his chest:
"OKIE." I ask for a photograph and, like every other genial character at
this cozy little gathering, Cal Meek gladly shares his tale.

"I taught at Arvin [California] High School for 35 years," Meek says,
"and in 1999 I took a group of students to a leadership conference in
Minneapolis, of all places. We would give students things to exchange
with other students—you know, just stuff to barter with as a way to get
them talking, trading. It's a good mixer. The Oklahoma delegation had
these shirts, and I wanted one."

He pauses for a second, squints in the late-summer California sun,
and swallows. "They were wearing them with pride, you see." Another

pause, but no loss of eye contact. "That's what got to me, the change in pride. They were *proud* to be called Okies, to call themselves Okies."

Now he looks away, scanning the flat cropland just beyond the schoolyard where hundreds of folks like him are gathered this Saturday morning. "It sure wasn't like that in 1939, 1940. For sure, I can tell you that."

On the surface, the annual Dust Bowl Festival is like any small-town fest. There are plentiful food booths—fried bologna sandwiches, biscuits and gravy, pit barbecue from Tomi's Country Café promising the "Best OKIE food in town" (again with the proud capitalization)—as well as local art on display and various tchotchkes for sale, from crafty straw hats to "Dust Bowl Migration & Route 66" aprons. A table for the chamber of commerce. Sign-ups for this and that. Oleta Kay Sprague Ham, granddaughter-in-law of Florence Thompson, the "Migrant Mother" in Dorothea Lange's famous photo, is signing copies of her new book. A band is on stage asking highly rhetorical questions between songs ("Anybody here like Merle Haggard?").

A few hundred feet east of the festival site—the Sunset School on the outskirts of Lamont, California, just south of Bakersfield—sits the Arvin Migrant Center, the reason for the gathering. That's its official, current designation, anyway, though you'll hear it called by many names: the Arvin Federal Government Camp, the Lamont Farm Labor Supply Center, the Sunset Labor Camp (the camp's address is on, no kidding, Sunset Boulevard), or its wider colloquialism: the Weedpatch Camp.

"Everyone calls the camp a different name," says Faye Holbert, a member of the Lamont Women's Club and a standout supporter of the camp's ongoing preservation effort. "They're always saying, 'No, *that's* not the right name…'"

Depending on the conversation, sometimes it's "Steinbeck's camp," since the novelist immortalized the place in *The Grapes of Wrath*. This is the real-life, makeshift town where the fictional Joads ended up, along with all the other thousands in the Dust Bowl diaspora of the 1930s.

Each year, on the third Saturday in October, the children of those Okies (and Arkies, Texans, Kansans, and more) gather for a little catch-up with compadres and cousins. Whether by blood or simple shared experience, everyone at the Dust Bowl Festival is family.

"We're looking for our cousins," says Mary Ann Witham as she walks through the gate. A dozen people I meet say the same thing. "I think he's a cousin of mine," Mary Garland says about a man I had just spoken with.

Garland and her husband moved back to Bakersfield last fall. For the previous 23 years, they'd been back home, just south of Fort Smith, Arkansas, growing chickens for Tyson. "But we came back, because this is where family is," she says. Without being asked, she produces family photos—but not the usual, color, Facebook-ubiquitous type. She instead fans out a hand of cracked, black-and-white snapshots, a few with scalloped white borders. One of them shows two teenage girls in denim overalls, scarves on their heads. "That's my friend and me at 16, working in the fields," she says.

She means those fields, over there, baking in today's SoCal sun. Garland's father, originally from Red Oak, Oklahoma, moved his family west from Arkansas in 1940. They wound up not at Weedpatch but another nearby workers' camp, where Garland met her husband. Today is their first visit to the Dust Bowl Festival. She felt compelled to come, even if her kids don't get it.

"We moved back here because, even though we're from Arkansas, this is where home really got to be for us," she says. "We went through hard times, and it's important to remember them, and why. Our kids have no clue how hard we worked. My son should really see this. We can tell them what we went through, but they should see it. It's the only way to really know how they got all they have today."

The demographics at the Dust Bowl Festival, though, appear highly stratified: lots of grandparents, lots of grandkids, not many in between. Jimmy Thompson is holding out for a change in the age range. Thompson helped found the festival in 1990, and he's been playing in bands and writing songs in the musical hotbed of nearby Bakersfield ever since his family settled in a tent at Weedpatch Camp in 1945. He's a lively, wiry gentleman, and he's convinced the inevitable passing of a generation with direct roots and experience at Weedpatch won't deflate a growing annual event.

"Folks like us, we're proud of what we had to work for, and our kids and our grandkids understand that," he says. "They still see it. Migrant workers aren't a thing of the past. The Arvin camp is full of them every summer. There's a whole young generation coming up that has plenty of experience with the kind of hard work and history rooted here. They know how to appreciate it, celebrate it.

"I wrote a song about this," Thompson says, then—because he obviously can't help himself—he suddenly breaks into the song:

> "Mom and Dad taught a way of life
> that good things don't come easy
> You've got to work for what you get
> and what you get will please you."

When Thompson's family arrived in California, they set up under some canvas in Weedpatch's "tent circle," and they were glad to be there. "At least this place had bathrooms," he says, "so you didn't have to go in a bush." We're standing next to one of the festival's food booths, hawking hunks of cornbread smothered in chili beans, as Thompson describes the lean times decades ago on this same piece of ground: "People would work for a spoon of flour and a cup of lard."

Faye Holbert's family arrived here in 1948. "We came out because all our siblings were here," she says. She worked for 22 years here at the Sunset School, an institution built by and for the very Okies the locals sought to isolate. "The school was built for the Dust Bowl people. Locals didn't want them. Really, that was fine by the Okies, because they took pride in their work and jumped right in. They helped build the school. They grew a garden; all the food in the cafeteria came out of that garden. They even built a swimming pool. There's pictures inside of kids digging the hole for the pool."

"He helped dig that pool," Betty Holliday says, pointing to her husband, Jack. They lived and worked at Weedpatch from 1941 to 1949. "That pool was something else."

Holbert chuckles. "Once the school got going with that pool," she says, "suddenly the locals were coming around, wondering if they could bring their kids. A peacemaker, that pool."

The swimming pool is gone, and that's a shame. The land around the Dust Bowl Festival is itself a hot, dusty basin. Driving to Bakersfield from the south—where I now live, in San Diego, just another Okie who moved West—brings you through big-town LA before creeping up the steady grades of the Sierra Pelona Mountains, a long and barren moonscape resembling grassy dunes. On the north side, the interstate dumps you into the central valley. There's a gas station, a Denny's, and a Ramada—beyond that, it's flat nothing as far as you can squint.

The trick is, though, you can't really see. The air over the whole southern end of the San Joaquin Valley is some of the most polluted in the country. Once again, in 2013, Bakersfield topped the American Lung Association's list of U.S. cities with the worst year-round air pollution.

Contrary to expectations, the thick brown haze hanging over the cropland here isn't creeping in from Los Angeles—where Woody Guthrie, in 1952, penned a short ditty called "Smoggy Old Smog" ("Smoggry oley smog why are ya here? / Smoggery oldey smog what bringsya here? / Ta choker down my towne fr'm th' middle of th' air? / What warnin are y' fr'm God?")—but rather from the Bay Area and, as reported in a recent study, all the way from China. Ozone produced by that county's voracious fossil fuel appetite "is transported at high altitude until it gets to the valley, where it takes a dive," according to an area air-pollution official quoted in *The Bakersfield Californian*, which publishes a lot of stories about air pollution.

Off the interstate, the drive into Bakersfield—Wheeler Ridge Road, which eventually becomes the Weedpatch Highway—passes fields full of an astonishing variety of produce, including some corn, several orchards, and a lot of grapes. The occasional tractor can be seen kicking up plumes of dry, tan dust, and that's part of the haze, too. By the end of the festival, my mouth was dry, and I could taste the dust.

"Our folks had their Dust Bowl," says Gary Richards, son of a Colorado farm worker at Weedpatch from 1940 to 1945, "and we've got this. Some days you can barely see the Tehachapi Mountains over there. My folks used to say this valley was starting to look like the one they left."

"It was mighty clear when we got here, a real picture," says Earl Shelton. "You could see every farm."

Shelton was 7 years old when he settled at Weedpatch in 1941. The family farm near Scipio, Oklahoma, simply dried up. When he couldn't water his crops, Shelton's dad, Tom, turned to selling skunk skins. The market for those, as you might imagine, stinks, so shortly after New Year's Day in 1941 Tom, a recent widower, packed his four sons into a rickety Model A Ford—the very embodiment of the Okie cliché—and started heading west on Route 66.

The tires came off the Ford near Seligman, Arizona. Tom managed to park the heap behind a gas station. For several days, Tom and his boys lived in the car. "I never went hungry, but I know my dad must have," Shelton recalls.

With his last nickel, Tom Shelton bought a cup of coffee and struck up a conversation with a rancher who offered Tom room and board for the family plus $2.50 a day—a fortune then—to dig a pond on his land 30 miles away. Eight weeks later, the Sheltons and a small nest-egg crossed into California and set up a tent among the sage brush on the edge of Weedpatch Camp.

Life at the camp was a relief. "Clean water, nice toilets, baseball, bands and dances on Saturday nights—we had the time of our lives, believe it," he says, brightening at the recollections. "Yessir, mighty nice."

Three of the camp's original Weedpatch buildings are preserved in the northeast corner of the fenced-in, gated Arvin Migrant Center, moved to this part of the site once becoming protected by the National Register of Historic Places in 1996. During the festival, a bus makes regular rounds between the school and the campsite. It's perfectly walkable, but—feel that sun, taste that dust—who'd want to?

The resituated buildings, awaiting further restoration, include the camp's library and post office. Outside the library stands a short granite monument, into which is embedded a plaque reading, "From the people of Oklahoma—the Okies—who found a home here and helped build California." Signed: Governor Frank Keating, 2002.

The big community building is the centerpiece—and the one that Okie kids still talk about. "We called it Magic Mountain," Earl Shelton says of the building, with its pitched roof and walls covered in bright green clapboard. The interior is about the size of the Cain's Ballroom in Tulsa, with a similarly sized stage on the far end. The floor is original, with surprisingly few creaks and sags. This is where the camp held most events, dances, concerts, suppers, church services, and self-governing meetings.

"One thing you notice when looking at [original] pictures from the camp and around the community building: There's no trash," Faye Holbert says. "One lady who was born in the camp said you didn't dare have things dirty. They'd call you out in those meetings and scold you. There were loudspeakers around the camp—they'd even say your name over the speakers."

The rest of the Arvin Migrant Center is still tidy today. While the Dust Bowl Festival celebrates its sepia-toned history, the old camp remains quite active in the present. From May to October each year, the camp provides the same service it has since it was built by the Farm Security Administration in 1936. Since 1965, the Arvin camp has been operated by the Housing Authority of the County of Kern. The tents and tin shacks are long gone, of course, replaced by 88 tidy wood-frame units—$11.50 a day for a two-bedroom duplex, $12 for three bedrooms, $12.50 for four.

Nearby states such as Arizona may seek to criminalize immigrants seeking work, but California's $43.5 billion-a-year farm industry still depends on a migrant labor force. Machinery can only do so much. Even in 2013, the grapes that make that sumptuous glass of California red wine you just photographed and posted on Facebook were plucked directly from the dusty vines by itinerant farmhands.

Just ask Mateo Martinez. He's 15, gangly, shy, wearing a Misfits t-shirt. While the tour-bus crew empties into the historic buildings, Mateo and his mother stand by the side of the road while she points out some of the existing, functioning buildings in the other direction.

"They [his parents] first came here in the '90s," Mateo says. "She says they picked celery and lived here two years." Work, wages, and some semblance of stability in the camp allowed Mateo's parents to save, move on, move up, buy a home, later work for and then start their own landscaping business further upstate.

I ask Mateo if he knows what an Okie is. He shoots me a withering, quizzical look; he does not. I mention they were a group of migrant workers who lived here before his parents did. "Did they build it?" he asks. In a way, I say, yes. He shrugs.

"That's cool," he says, and he looks back toward the neat rows of houses. "Otherwise, I guess I wouldn't be here."

THE OTHER MOTHER ROAD

An exploration of a Route 66 once off-limits to black people and
the book they used to navigate it.

By *Michael Wallis*

Pour yourself a sipping drink and get comfortable. I am going
to tell you a story. It's about a postal worker named Victor Green and
his Green Book, a very special publication that provided invaluable and
sometimes even life-saving assistance to thousands of disenfranchised
open-road travelers. Published annually for almost 30 years, this guidebook for the nation's highways, including America's Main Street at the
time, Route 66, was as essential to those who relied on it as the gasoline
in the tank and good tread on the tires.

This is a road story that has seldom been told. It needs to be and I
am grateful for the opportunity to share it with you.

Let me begin by saying that I am a true son of Route 66, born and
bred on the old road. I also believe in the value of understanding the
entire history of the highway. We simply must know and understand
our past—the good, bad, and sometimes ugly—before we can manage
the present and aspire to a future.

So I search the road as it is today, but also I continually go back to
its past in order that I may preserve and protect this legendary highway for the future. That means I learn from the various layers, the dis-
tinct incarnations of Route 66—starting with its birth in the Roar-
ing Twenties, the bittersweet "Dirty Thirties," when the rains stopped

and an economic downturn that was so devastating we still refer to it as the Great Depression struck this nation. I learn from the war years when the highway served the nation so well, and, of course, I also turn to the so-called heyday of the road before the many new interstate highways came along. And I take stock of those years when Route 66 sank into a period of limbo before we were able to revive the old path of varicose concrete and asphalt and bring the Mother Road back in this ongoing renaissance.

Let's go back for a few minutes and revisit one of the highway's incarnations. Come back with me to that period after war's end—the time that made up the so-called glory years of Route 66.

Come back with me to June of 1952. It most definitely was another time, another place. I was seven years old, and I recall neighbors in their backyards searching the night sky for flying saucers. Newspapers offered the latest reports on labor strife and atomic tests. The Korean conflict raged. Threat of a polio epidemic gripped the land. Out of Wisconsin, a vitriolic Senator Joe McCarthy, blinded by rancor and fear, prepared for his insidious Communist witch-hunt.

Despite the discord and apprehension, all was right with the world if you happened to be me—a kid growing up in Missouri within easy striking distance of Route 66.

Although Harry Truman was not running for another term of office, our family was proud that the Show Me State's favorite son was still president of the United States. Down at our neighborhood theater, my band of friends felt Gary Cooper was worth every penny of admission portraying the stoic lawman in *High Noon*. Our television favorites included *I Love Lucy*, *The Ernie Kovacs Show*, and *The Adventures of Ozzie and Harriet*. We never failed to miss *Dragnet*, the cop show starring Jack Webb as the poker-faced Sergeant Joe Friday.

Much to my delight, plastic vinylite swimming pools and *Mad* comics made their debut that summer. So did the mechanical lawnmower. Most of my attention, however, turned to Stan "The Man" Musial. The St. Louis Cardinal slugger was on his way to winning the National League batting crown with a hefty .336 average.

I can see the blimps and skywriting planes flying over my neighborhood. I can smell the thick white clouds of mosquito spray wafting from the trucks slowly rolling down the streets. I remember uniformed service station attendants pumping gasoline, washing bug-splattered windshields, and filling tires with pressurized air.

Best of all, I recall, June meant it was summertime. School was out for three whole months. Everyone went on vacation. If you were a kid of summer, you only worried about capturing more lighting bugs than your pal, explaining grass stains on your good pants, and trying to collect pop bottles for refunds to buy baseball cards and firecrackers for the Fourth of July.

On most June days just after dawn the air remained cool. But as the sun climbed higher, the dreaded St. Louis humidity was already sneaking out of the damp lawn. Thank god for attic fans, sun-brewed ice tea, and Mr. Busch's brewery.

Out in the garage, my dad packed suitcases, thermos bottles, ice chests, road maps, ball gloves, fishing gear, and all the essentials needed to keep a family going for two whole weeks. Finally, Dad had his pride and joy—the shiny green Plymouth he called the "Green Monster"—loaded and ready.

Mom had checked every item off the list. Our dog was in the kennel, the parakeet resided with friends, and the milkman was alerted. Neighbors vowed to water the tomatoes and take in the mail and papers. My mom got off every birthday card and paid every bill. It was time for us to take to the open road.

Just the act of "getting there" was an important part of our vacation experience. We did not want to lose a single moment so we made the drive an indispensable component of the overall trip. There was an assortment of man-made and natural attractions to visit, tourist traps to survive, detours to avoid, and truck stop meals to consume.

———————

Within a couple of decades people would be more interested in their final destination than in the process of traveling. Families would fly off to tennis resorts and dude ranches and amusement parks. They would take the impersonal interstate highways that might as well be airport runways to one of the countless look-alike attractions dotting the nation. "Getting there" would not matter anymore. That was not the case in 1952.

In 1952, and throughout the heyday of Route 66, Dad only had to start the engine. When he turned the key of the Green Monster it was official—the vacation had started. We did not squander any time. Every minute counted.

Soon Dad had the entire family out on U. S. Route 66. We cranked down the windows. Black-eyed Susans and Queen Anne's lace lining the road flashed by as Dad mashed the gas pedal. Everyone else tried to figure out when the first pit stop would occur.

The voices of Peggy Lee, Eddie Fisher, Teresa Brewer, and Hank Williams poured from the radio. The Mother Road beckoned. I dreamed of reptile farms, Indian artifacts, and outlaw hideouts that waited down the highway. My mouth watered for cheeseburger platters and thick chocolate malts. The fantasy had begun. My hunger for the road and all that lay ahead grew with each passing mile.

Traveling the highway excited us whether our family headed east, across the Mississippi River into Illinois and inched up Route 66 through the "Land of Lincoln" to Springfield or Chicago, or drove west out of St. Louis. Route 66 ambled down the Ozark Plateau and pushed on to Kansas, Oklahoma, Texas, New Mexico, Arizona, all the way to the California shore.

In either direction we found plenty of adventure. Nothing was predictable. The potential for an escapade lurked around every curve and bend in the road.

Maybe you have similar memories.

We tend to look back through rose-colored glasses and call that time the "Good Old Days." Life was easy for many of us in the '50s. Life was as sweet as truck stop pie, at least it was for me—a white boy without a care in the world from a middle-class family living in a comfortable home in the heartland.

Now, of course, I know the cold, hard truth. Now I realize those days were not really so good; I only remember them that way. The main reason many of us considered those times the Good Old Days is simple. It comes down to technology. People didn't know what was happening everywhere in the country and the world. They were uninformed for the most part, especially in rural America. There was no 24-hour news cycle worldwide. They were not bombarded with news and views. There was no Internet. No iPhones.

You cannot restore myths or turn back the clock to a dream that only existed for certain Americans. To live solely in the past is to live in complete denial.

Perhaps the good old days aren't good; they are just old. The old wisdom-keepers told us not to ask why the old days were better than these, because such a question arises, not from wisdom, but from amnesia. Some of us have selective memories. We tend to believe in cliché, romanticize the past—our own past—and edit out any bad memories.

And what about those broken and frightened tenant farmers and Dust Bowlers driving down the road to what they had been told was the land of milk and honey? What about the Indian people or the others of color trying to eke out a living? What of them? What if I had been a six-year-old African-American boy cruising down Route 66, or any highway in the nation, back then—would I look back on that time as "Good Old Days"? I doubt it.

Back then, not only in the Jim Crow Deep South, but also everywhere in the land—including Oklahoma—if you were a person of color, you lived in another America. One that had no dreams. No hope. You could not eat in the same building or shop in the same store as white folks. You could not get gasoline from a white-owned pump or even think about staying in even the most basic white-owned lodging. You could not sit with white people in the Art Deco Tulsa train station and wait for a train. There was a separate place for you and your kind.

Many of us who have an abiding interest in Route 66 realize that because the highway is arguably the most famous roadway in the nation, and perhaps the world, we have an obligation to share the entire story of the old highway we love.

In the main, today's astonishing revival of interest in the Mother Road has overlooked the inequities and the negative history that certainly transpired along the road's shoulders and continues in some ways to this day.

There is ample reason to question the romanticizing of Route 66. There also is reason to stop avoiding that dark side of the highway story that all too often has been swept beneath the proverbial and convenient carpet.

Remember that this highway—our highway—is a true mirror of the nation. Like all roads, this road and what takes place on this road reflects our society and culture. Now that includes the good, the bad, the ugly, the holy, the shades of gray, and the truth of life. That has always been the case. That has always been a fact. That will never change.

———————

It was true when the highway was born back in 1926—when our beloved road, like all other roads of the time, was less than hospitable particularly if the traveler happened to be black or red or brown or anything other than lily white.

It was true when great posses of Dust Bowl pilgrims, refugees, and disenfranchised souls poured onto the road. All of them headed west, following the scent of oranges and lemons and escaping the harsh reality of economic depression, drought, and foreclosure. All of them headed to the San Joaquin Valley, to Bakersfield, to Fresno, to San Bernardino, to Los Angeles. All of them headed to the growing fields, the ripe orchards and groves, the lush vineyards, the factories and airplane plants, and the sunny beaches.

Theirs was far from being an idyllic journey on Route 66. Our highway may have earned the title Mother Road, thanks to Mr. Steinbeck, but sometimes—and too often—she could be an abusive Mother, a delinquent and uncaring parent. Ask the hordes of Okies and Arkies, the dirt-poor tenant farmers, the unemployed city workers who were billy-clubbed, spat upon, shunned, cursed, abused, cheated, and lied to by others blinded by fear and ignorance and hatred—bigots worried only about themselves and their own kind.

Read *The Grapes of Wrath*. Read every single word of it. Memorize the story of the fictional Joads.

Like so many others these were ordinary people striving to preserve their humanity in the face of social and economic depression. Like no other book, Steinbeck's novel provides a portrait of the bitter conflict between the powerful and the powerless. It truly captures the horrors of the Great Depression as it probes the very nature of equality and justice in this land.

Look at the striking and all-too-real photographic portraits created by the incomparable Dorothea Lange—images that document the lives of poor people on the long highway; images of Dust Bowl refu-

gees, of children near starvation while in the midst of California's ver-
dant fields. Look at the images of a haggard mother, a Madonna of the
highway, looking four times her age; of homes fashioned of cardboard
and rubbish.

Listen to the songs, the poetry of Woody Guthrie. He was never
afraid to confront the injustice of those years, to question authority,
to standup for those who could not stand up for themselves. To make
tough decisions in tough times.

But Woody was lucky. Even when he was down and out and busted
like the folks he sang about, at least he was the right color. Ironically,
only a few years later, the late great Nat King Cole, the man with the
velvet voice that helped immortalize the highway by singing Bobby
Troup's "Get Your Kicks," found that out. Like millions of African Americans, Hispanics, American Indians and others, Cole for way too long
would not be able to check into even a modest tourist court or dine in
a greasy spoon on the Mother Road or any other road in this country.

As a boy, I saw the "No Colored" signs at gas stations on my Route
66 just as I did on the roads of the Deep South. I also saw signs in cafe
windows declaring, "No dogs, No Bums, No Indians," and only yards
away a Native American craftsman sold his hand-fashioned art from
the sidewalk. Black families traveling America's byways packed their
own food and often slept in their vehicles. They didn't get their kicks
on Route 66—or at least the kind of kicks I was getting as a youngster
or a few years later as a hitchhiking Marine. At highway stops such as
the Rock Cafe in Stroud, Oklahoma, during the '30s, '40s, '50s, and
into the '60s, black travelers went to the back door to get their food to
go. None of them walked inside.

In one resort Ozarks burg, the local commercial club proudly handed out brochures touting their town. They boasted of:

- Cool Summers
- Mild Winters
- Pretty Homes
- Schools and Churches

- Lodges and Societies
- Health and Happiness

They also bragged that their heaven on earth had:

- No Mosquitos
- No Blizzards
- No Malaria
- No Drouth
- No Negroes

To many white, middle- and upper-class travelers, Route 66 symbolized the most positive aspects of American society—freedom, progress, and economic possibility. But to the minorities who encountered racism, prejudice, and exploitation along the road, Route 66 embodied a much darker version of American history.

Thank god for that little guidebook I wrote about at the start of this story. That little book that probably saved a good many lives.

———————

Starting in 1936 and every year after until 1964, when the Civil Rights Act rendered it obsolete, that straightforward guide helped African Americans travel throughout the country in a safe and comfortable manner. A Harlem postal worker and activist named Victor H. Green published it. He named it *The Negro Motorist Green Book*. Some folks called it the Negro Travelers' Green Book, but it was mostly known as The Green Book. Every cover bore a quotation from Mark Twain: "Travel is fatal to prejudice."

Modeling his guide on Jewish travel guides, Victor Green carefully listed state-by-state hotels, motels, tourist homes, restaurants, gas stations, beauty and barbershops, and other businesses that would serve African Americans. It quickly became known as "the bible of every Negro traveler in the 1950s and early 1960s." Any black family or individual embarking on a trip did not dare leave home with a Green Book.

For many years, with Howard Johnson being the sole nationwide chain where blacks could eat and sleep, and Esso (later Exxon) being the only major fuel outlet actually offering franchises to blacks, the pickings were very slim. In 1955, for example, 3,500 white motels would allow dogs to stay in guest rooms, but less than 50 stated they would even consider housing any black travelers. During this same period, an Oklahoma motel operator reluctantly allowed a black family to stay at his motel for two days if they agreed to "pass" as Mexicans. There are several reports that in 1961 so many black tourists along Route 66 in Illinois were refused restaurant service that they took to bringing their own food and eating in their cars rather than chance being embarrassed. Undoubtedly, that accounts for why most editions of the Green Book listed nothing between Chicago and Springfield as well as nothing between Springfield and East St. Louis. There were also large gaps for Missouri, Texas, and New Mexico.

As far as Oklahoma, most Route 66 listings were businesses in the black sections of Oklahoma City and Tulsa, a bit better than Arizona's long stretch of the Mother Road where there was not a single accommodation for black travelers. Of course, many black travelers detoured to towns with significant black populations such as the all-black Boley, or else Muskogee and Okmulgee.

Prior to the horrific 1921 Greenwood massacre in Tulsa, most often called a "race riot," that thriving African American neighborhood provided comfort and hospitality for many blacks traveling through this part of the country. Even though the white mob burned most of Greenwood to the ground, by the late 1940s numerous black-owned businesses had sprung from the ashes and some found their way into the Green Book. One of the primary lodging choices was the Hotel Small on Archer Street, popular with travelers including such celebrities as Louis Armstrong, who stayed there during an appearance in Tulsa. The 1949 edition of the Green Book featured other Tulsa businesses including the Warren Hotel, the Red Wing, and McHunt Hotels, all on Greenwood Avenue, and the Royal on Archer Avenue. W.H. Smith on Greenwood and C. U. Nederland on Elgin Street operated two of the best tourist homes. Black travelers in need of some tonsorial care were directed to Swindall's with its crew of friendly barbers.

Outside of larger cities such as Tulsa, the notorious "sundown towns" had to be avoided at all costs. These towns could be found across the nation, especially in the South and Midwest. The ominous name came from the fact that all of them prohibited any African Americans from even being within the city limits after sundown. Most of them usually posted warning signs to that effect. Often times, the weary black traveler found it best to just keep going and not risk the consequences of being discovered in a town where "his kind" was not welcome.

———————

Thankfully, the Green Book finally outlived its usefulness. Yet injustice, racism, and sexism in the nation and along this highway have not vanished. Far from it. Just look around. Look at our highway today. Read the blatantly racist signs on motels and other businesses proclaiming in great big letters "American Owned." These are the code words, these are signs erected by the small-minded and the mean-spirited, by those who wear their religion and their patriotism on their sleeve and on their bumper. Signs that serve no good purpose except to divide us and slap us in the face.

It is yet another tactic to call attention to a racial stereotype—in this case the targets are the East Indian-operated motels. "Don't go there, a raghead runs the place," or, "I walked in and the smell of curry almost knocked me down."

To these people I say: Get over it. Don't generalize. Don't stereotype. Try the curry. Who knows, you might like it.

Remember the many reputable motel owners and operators from India, Pakistan, and Asia who are doing their dead-level best to provide service in their adopted homeland. Some are good operators and some are not, just like every other place on the road. Many of them are American citizens. Most are well educated and as professional as anyone doing business on Route 66.

Before you decide to boycott all the Indian-run motels and businesses do yourself a favor and spend some time in one of the properties on old Route 66. They are fine examples of just how important all people are to our historic road.

Bear in mind the words of advice offered by Georgia O'Keeffe: "Where I was born and how I lived is unimportant. It is what I have done with where I have been that should be of interest."

Reject the ignorant and the ill informed. Turn your backs on the purveyors of hatred. Seek out the good in all people. Conform your actions to the good of all others. Choose the high road. It takes strength and discipline to choose that path. Take a step in its direction—one step at a time, one day at a time.

And bear in mind that the Mother Road remains the center of memorable change, disputes, compromise, triumphs, and controversies. It is so many things.

Route 66 is big cities and tiny towns. It is rich farmland, Ozark forests, vast prairies and rangeland, high and low desert, great mountains, mighty streams. It is a road for red necks and blue bloods. It is six "red states" bookended by two "blue states," so the color runs purple. Flood, earthquake, fire, and killer tornadoes have tempered it and its people. Route 66 is the eight states it traverses and bits and pieces of 42 more. It is American, through and through.

The highway has yielded plenty of saints and also a good many sinners. It is not just black and white but shades of gray and all the colors of the rainbow and then some.

The Route 66 story is both bitter and sweet. A microcosm of the nation, the old road has plenty of scar tissue, much to be ashamed of and much to brag about, as well as a bright future. It is an unfinished story—a work in progress. It always will be.

Enjoy the journey.

Editor's note: Portions of this essay were previously published elsewhere.

STEPS TO NOWHERE

Twenty-five years ago, Tulsa still had one traditional, mixed-use pre-World War II neighborhood. The city tore it down to make way for college classrooms that will never be built.

By *Michael Bates*

JUST NORTH OF DOWNTOWN TULSA there is a vast empty area, about a half-mile long by a third of a mile wide. This wasteland is punctuated only by the Salvation Army's compound on the south end and a 1970s-vintage elementary school at the north end. The Oklahoma State University-Tulsa campus borders it on the east.

Superimposed on the empty, green space is a grid of seldom-used streets, each one paralleled by a pair of buckled or overgrown sidewalks, interrupted periodically by the stub of a driveway. Where there is a steep enough incline from the sidewalk to the middle of the block, there are sets of stone or concrete steps, leading up the rise to bare ground. At the steepest inclines, tilting, buckling walls try to keep the hill from spilling out onto the street.

MISTAKEN IDENTITY

The observer notes that this place is north of downtown and remembers that it was north of downtown in 1921 that a white mob invaded, looted, and burned an African-American neighborhood to the ground.

Ethiopian artist Eyakem Gulilat photographed this empty land and the concrete steps to nowhere, intending his installation to be a record of the physical legacy of the 1921 Race Riot. "Using photography as a constant witness, I observe the changes that took place in this location through the last 100 years and how the place holds memory of this great tragedy. The land is an unbiased witness to the lives and events from the past..."

The land is an unbiased witness, but the steps and sidewalks tell us only that once there were homes here—not when they were built, what they looked like, when they went away, or why they went away.

The regularity of the boundary and the thorough cleansing that took place within does not suggest the chaotic destruction of an inflamed mob. The land bears the mark of an officially planned and methodically executed purge—more *Kelo v. New London* than Kristallnacht.

There are other unbiased witnesses: federal census records, annual city directories, fire insurance maps showing the shape, height, and material of every building, aerial photos, title deeds, subdivision plats. Created at the time for various practical purposes, these records combine as an unintentional documentary of a neighborhood's history, providing a context for these ruins on a hill overlooking downtown.

There are also living witnesses whose fond memories and precious photographs put flesh on the bones of the official records. They are senior citizens now, but as children in the middle of the 20th century, they bounded down these steps heading to school or church or summertime explorations with their pals. They rode their bikes down these streets in the pre-dawn darkness delivering the morning paper. Walking these sidewalks, they carried groceries home from the corner store. Where there is now only a treeless stretch of grass, they drank chocolate shakes at a drugstore soda fountain.

These witnesses tell a story. Until 25 years ago, there was a neighborhood here. Until 10 years ago, a few buildings remained.

THE STORY OF THE STEPS

The story of the steps to nowhere is not a tragedy on the order of the 1921 looting and burning of the African-American community down the hill and a half-mile to the east. It is not a tragedy on the order of the

City of Tulsa's federally funded demolition of the neighborhood that the African-American community had rebuilt from the ashes of 1921.

It is a tragedy of relentless bureaucracy, faulty projections, and bad urban design. Even as cities across America were rediscovering the value of the traditional neighborhood with jobs, shops, schools, and churches within walking distance of homes, Tulsa was destroying one of the few traditional mixed-use neighborhoods still in its possession, for the sake of a goal that vanished before the destruction was even complete.

At the beginning of the 20th century, Tulsa grew from sleepy whistle-stop to oil-fired boomtown. The population, 50 times bigger in just 20 years, spilled out into new neighborhoods in every direction.

On the highlands to the north, past the Frisco and the Katy tracks, seven new subdivisions were laid out, their streets forming a seamless grid and a single neighborhood. Asked where they lived, the residents of this new neighborhood would simply say "the Northside" or "up on the hill."

The Northside wasn't downtown, wasn't Owen Park, off to the west, and it especially wasn't the district down the hill to the east, known variously as the East End, Greenwood, Little Africa, or more derogatory names. The Northside spanned from Easton Street on the south to Marshall Street on the north to Osage Drive and the Tulsa Country Club on the west. The eastern border came up Detroit Avenue as far as Haskell Street (known today as John Hope Franklin Boulevard), then traced around the crest of Sunset Hill.

Early city directories documented Tulsa's racial geography by marking certain residents' names with a "(c)" for "colored." The Northside was a white neighborhood, with the exception of a few residents of servants' quarters over the detached garages of the grander homes. In the 1920 directory, every name on the east, odd-numbered side of Detroit Avenue is followed by a (c); on the west, even-numbered side, none are.

The 1918 "Aero View of Tulsa" shows most of our Northside neighborhood in the foreground, and captures it in a state of near-complete development, filled with one- and two-story frame houses, mainly of the craftsman and foursquare styles. Standing atop its namesake hill between Easton and Fairview is the city's standpipe, or water tower, and, on the hill's western flank at Boston Avenue, the impressive two-story

Sequoyah School with its domed bell tower, opened as Northside School in 1906. A block further west, at Main and Easton, is Tigert Memorial Methodist Church, the first church in the neighborhood; in just six years it would be replaced by the Ku Klux Klan's Beno Hall. Next to Tigert Church on the north is Fire Station No. 2, built in 1909.

At the five-point intersection where Boulder, Main, and Haskell come together, where downtown's railroad-tilted grid meets the compass-aligned streets that dominate the rest of the city, the picture shows a scattering of brick apartment buildings and stores. There are two hospitals—infirmaries, really—on Boulder between Easton and Fairview: Cinnabar, in a large house across from two-story brick Morningside, forerunner of Hillcrest.

On the right-hand side (south and west) there are the first few buildings of Osage School, one of the first built to Tulsa's innovative, incremental "unit plan," opened in 1913. (Lee School and the former Lincoln School are surviving examples of the type.)

The school is flanked by the grand mansions of the country-club district, with the open space of Owen Park and the Tulsa Country Club beyond. The tracks running down the center of Cheyenne belong to the Tulsa Street Railway, connecting the Northside to downtown via Cameron Street and Main Street with a trolley car every seven-and-a-half minutes from early morning until late at night.

Off the edge of the picture to the north is another new unit-plan school: Emerson, between King and Latimer on the east side of Boston Avenue, had opened its doors on January 5, 1916.

THE 1920S AND THE RIOT

Around this time C.W. "Doc" Medlock established his home and his optometry practice just north of Standpipe Hill at 618 N. Cincinnati. (N. Cincinnati was renamed Martin Luther King Jr. Boulevard in 2012.) Doc made glasses for his white neighbors on the hill and the African-American residents of the valley to his east.

On June 1, 1921, Detroit Avenue, the dividing line between the races, became the front line of the battle, just a block east of Doc Medlock's place. Years later, his wife, Ollie, would tell their grandson Chris (who would grow up to be a Tulsa city councilor) how Doc sat up all night on the front porch with a shotgun, prepared to defend his home against anyone who might try to attack.

But the 1921 Race Riot barely grazed the Northside. National Guardsmen were called to the north edge of Sunset Hill, west of the present-day Pioneer Plaza tower, to deal with a report of black riflemen at the base of the hill firing up into the white-owned homes on the crest of the hill. The guardsmen had heard a rumor that the shots had killed a white woman, and two guardsmen who came to investigate were slightly wounded under fire. The guardsmen returned fire with a few shots from a decrepit machine gun and then moved down hill in pursuit of the riflemen.

That is the only report of riot violence reaching the neighborhood of steps to nowhere; all of the buildings "up on the hill" survived the riot. Down the hill, the Greenwood residents successfully fought a city plan to convert the burned-out district to an industrial center, and then rebuilt their homes, stores, and churches. They weren't able, half a century later, to stop a city plan that leveled all but a handful of buildings in the name of "slum clearance" and "urban renewal."

DECADES OF STABILITY

New neighborhoods sprang up farther north, so our neighborhood is better described from this point forward as the Near Northside. The Near Northside changed over the next 50 years, but redevelopment happened gradually, one lot at a time. Small apartment buildings, filling stations, and mom-and-pop stores mixed in with the homes and schools. The neighborhood had a few churches, a Jewish community center, and a couple of beer joints.

Tulsans who spent their childhoods in the Near Northside during the 1940s, 1950s, and early 1960s remember it as an idyllic place.

As a five-year-old, Bill Leighty (today a realtor and former planning commissioner) walked on his own to Curry Drug at Main and Latimer, where he could browse comic books or enjoy a cherry Coke at the fountain. A striped pole on a small house behind Curry's marked Bert Daniels' barber shop.

The 50-foot-deep pits that the brick factory had dug into the side of Sunset Hill, declared off-limits by responsible parents, were magnets for the adventurous young person, where Martin Reidy (the last homeowner to leave in 2004) hunted for scorpions, tarantulas, and horny toads.

For spending money, a kid could mow lawns or deliver handbills for the corner grocery. If you shopped at Romney's on Main and needed help getting your groceries home, Johnnie Cherblanc (a real estate executive nowadays) would carry your bags for a quarter tip.

A kid didn't depend on grown-ups to get around. Mike Littrell, who lived near Boulder and Fairview in the early '60s, would walk to the Page-Glencliff dairy store at Boston and Haskell for a 10-cent scoop of banana nut, ride his bike downtown, or take the bus to see the Oilers play ball.

But this beloved neighborhood was doomed. At mid-century, the experts believed that government could and must reorganize America's cities. The science was settled: Traditional neighborhoods, with their mixture of homes and shops and jobs, small lots, old homes, and dense street grids, were insalubrious and a cause of poverty. New neighborhoods on the edge of the city would be designed in accordance with modern, scientific planning theories. Residential areas would be uncontaminated by nearby businesses. Expressways, modeled after Hitler's autobahns, would speed residents between their shiny new suburbs and downtown jobs and shopping.

A new tool called "urban renewal" would be used to level and redevelop obsolete neighborhoods that didn't match the scientific model. Uncle Sam generously offered $9 to match every local dollar toward urban renewal and expressway construction. States authorized cities to create the planning commissions and urban renewal authorities required to receive Washington's largesse.

For some local leaders, it was a happy coincidence that free money from Washington gave them the power and resources to shunt lucrative demolition and construction contracts to political allies, to boost demand for new homes and shopping centers in the suburbs for their developer friends, and to relocate undesirable ethnicities away from the city center. The Germans kept their autobahns away from their cities and towns; city leaders in America saw that they could be used to eliminate outdated neighborhoods or at least wall them off from the central business district.

About the time that Jane Jacobs and her allies were successfully defending New York's traditional neighborhoods, Tulsa was pushing ahead with modern, scientific planning, as fast as state law would allow, forming the Tulsa Metropolitan Area Planning Commission in 1955 and the Tulsa Urban Renewal Authority in 1959.

TMAPC's 1957 Comprehensive Plan defined the model suburban square mile: a school surrounded by houses on large lots, connected by winding streets and cul-de-sacs. Shopping centers on the periphery, carefully segregated from the houses, had plenty of parking spaces and needed them because there was no direct path from home to store.

The map of "blight, sprawl, and renewal areas" in TMAPC's Preliminary Land Use Plan claimed that over 30 percent of the buildings on nearly every block of the Near Northside were "dilapidated," and the neighborhood was "needing treatment."

The 1957 expressway plan connected an "Inner Dispersal Loop" hub around downtown to distant, growing suburban neighborhoods, the spokes cutting through older, inner neighborhoods.

Oklahoma law authorized cities to condemn property for "blight," a condition so expansively defined that it could apply to any building that wasn't brand new. An entire neighborhood could be condemned as blighted, no matter how well-kept each individual property might be, if their arrangement didn't fit the new suburban standard.

The grand metropolitan plans began to nibble away at the neighborhood in the late '60s, when the state began clearing land to make way for I-244. Cincinnati was widened and cut through the middle of Standpipe Hill to connect to the new freeway. In the '70s, the western fringe of the neighborhood was cleared and Osage Elementary School was demolished to make way for the Osage (now L. L. Tisdale) Expressway.

Now out of sight and out of mind for city leaders downtown, the area headed into a decline. Stores that sold new items became resale shops. Drug dealers and prostitutes roamed the streets.

In 1975, Emerson Elementary was demolished and replaced with a new building, part of the school district's "magnet school" desegregation strategy. TURA cleared four whole blocks—46 single-family homes, four duplexes, seven apartment buildings, and a beer joint—and the city closed Boston and King through the new school's "superblock" campus.

Urban renewal plans of this period called for the clearance of nearly all non-residential uses and multi-family housing, with commercial uses permitted only along Denver, south of Fairview. The city's policy was to eliminate the mixed-use quality that set the Near Northside apart from other neighborhoods. Given time, those former commercial sites might have been filled with single-family homes.

Tulsa's pursuit of state-funded higher education would change everything for the Near Northside. In 1982, the dream of a free-standing Tulsa State University gave way to an awkward compromise called the University Center at Tulsa (UCAT). Langston University, Oklahoma State University, University of Oklahoma, and Northeastern State University would offer graduate and upper-level undergraduate courses toward a degree from one of the four schools, on a 200-acre campus to be provided by the city.

The city chose the Greenwood District, north of I-244 and east of Detroit, as the heart of the new campus. The 84.6 acres had been home, in 1960, to about 2,200 people and dozens of businesses, but it had been leveled by the Model Cities urban renewal program and sat empty save for two churches and a house. The plan to replace Greenwood with high-intensity residential and commercial development had gone nowhere.

In 1985, the City of Tulsa established the University Center at Tulsa Authority (UCATA) to acquire, improve, and maintain a campus on behalf of the four colleges. A firm drew up a master plan, and City of Tulsa voters approved funds for the first academic buildings, which opened in 1988. In 1986, the Tulsa Development Authority, successor to TURA, had signed a lengthy development agreement with UCATA, requiring the land be used for a public university and for development to occur in a timely fashion, and transferred the initial campus area to UCATA.

The remaining 115 acres would come from the Near Northside neighborhood. The homes east of Cincinnati atop Sunset Hill had already been cleared. Urban renewal plans were updated in the late '80s to reflect the new direction. East Haskell (now John Hope Franklin Boulevard) would be connected to West Fairview as a peripheral road, and every other street in the acquisition area (Jasper south to the IDL) would be closed. Pedestrians would be given a tunnel under the new road east of the former site of Boulder Avenue. In the early '90s, the

Tulsa Development Authority, successor to TURA, began voluntary buyouts of Near Northside homes.

Two parts of the Near Northside would be spared. On the west fringe, Denver and Cheyenne avenues had been added to the National Register of Historic Places in 1980 as the Brady Heights Historic District. Emerson School's superblock protected the homes and the Boydell Apartments to its north; the commercial buildings were cleared in accordance with the earlier plan.

A 1990 historic preservation report recommended adding the rest of the Near Northside to the Brady Heights Historic District. City authorities had already sealed the area's fate; the report was shelved.

UCAT BECOMES OSU-TULSA

While TDA was relentlessly bulldozing homes for UCAT, UCAT was mutating into something very different from a campus that boosters confidently projected would have 20,000 students by 2000.

The consortium blew apart in 1998. OU-Tulsa moved to 41st Street and Yale Avenue. Broken Arrow built a campus for NSU. Langston wanted its own building in the UCAT acquisition area. OSU-Tulsa was all that remained of UCAT.

In 1999, OSU-Tulsa unveiled a grandiose master plan. With only 4,200 students enrolled, the 20,000-student target was rescheduled from 2000 to 2020. The plan, still on display in an upstairs lounge, shows the campus sprawling across all 200 acres. Academic buildings would sit on a series of five terraces leading from the original campus buildings up Sunset Hill to a new campus library on the summit, replacing Pioneer Plaza and Sunset Plaza Apartments.

Campus housing and a wellness center would go west of Cincinnati. The urban grid would be replaced with winding suburban streets and cul-de-sacs. For the complete college experience, OSU-Tulsa even planned to build houses for fraternities and sororities.

In April 2004, TDA demolished the last three homes in the neighborhood. By the end of 2005, Fire Station No. 2 and a few nearby industrial buildings were gone, the final step to nowhere.

OSU-Tulsa's latest master plan, from 2011, a Google map superimposed with Arial type and shaded polygons, has already been overtaken by events.

The Oklahoma School for the Visual and Performing Arts will be at the former Roosevelt Junior High and won't need eight acres south of Emerson School. The Tulsa City-County Library is renovating Central Library, rather than relocate to the western half of Standpipe Hill. Vision2's defeat in November 2012 eliminated funding for a new classroom building and student center. The future of the Millennium Center, a demonstration site for sustainability concepts, is up in the air. OSU-Tulsa caters to commuting locals; on-campus housing won't be needed. The Salvation Army, Pioneer Plaza, and Sunset Plaza Apartments won't be moving. OSU-Tulsa doesn't need the land to move forward with its plans, and there are no funds for relocation.

A technology and research park on Sunset Hill between MLK and Pioneer Plaza is still on the table. OSU-Tulsa would build and lease office and lab space to high-tech companies.

Only the "Hill Top Gateway" on Standpipe Hill has been realized. Without stairs or windows, the tower, which stirs uncomfortable memories of snipers firing into Greenwood from that same hill, serves only as a big sign to alert I-244 drivers to OSU-Tulsa's existence.

STEPS BACK TO SOMEWHERE

In the 15 years since OSU-Tulsa's first and most elaborate master plan, enrollment has shrunk from about 4,200 to 2,842 for spring 2014. Langston-Tulsa has 356 students. That's a long way from 20,000 by 2020.

The demand for higher ed in Tulsa may be as great as UCAT boosters expected, but students have found more convenient and cost-effective means to meet their goals. Tulsa branches of private and for-profit colleges and dozens of online options cater to the needs of non-traditional students.

Even OSU's own online course options are competing with OSU-Tulsa. For the fall 2013 semester, the school offered the "Get Here" tuition waiver—$250 for students who took all their courses on campus. A poster promoting the plan pointed out that on-campus students would also avoid extra online class fees.

The wasteland was created for a university, but it isn't owned by a university. The Oklahoma A&M Regents own the north academic building and the auditorium (but not the administrative building), and they own the site of the Technology Center west of Elgin. As Langston's governing body, they also own the Langston-Tulsa campus. The remainder of the 200 acres—including the Near Northside wasteland and OSU-Tulsa's massive parking lots—still belongs to UCATA, a trust of the City of Tulsa governed by six trustees who are appointed by the mayor and confirmed by the City Council to five-year terms.

The terms of the land's transfer from TDA to UCATA allow for the land to revert if it's not needed for higher ed.

Despite its total destruction, the Near Northside's wasteland has never been replatted. The grid of streets and parcels that served as the womb for its development 100 years ago could be the matrix for its regeneration, one lot at a time. Tulsa's new comprehensive plan calls for zoning tools that could be used to recreate the style of homes and mixture of uses that characterized the neighborhood in its heyday.

Perhaps someday, the steps to nowhere will lead somewhere once again.

THE INDIAN OF THEIR DREAMS

From San Francisco to Oklahoma, following the journey of
James Earle Fraser's 'End of the Trail.'

By *Mark Brown*

Regardless of the scars I carry from all that has taken place
since we undertook the project, I still experience the same
wonderfully warm feeling when I gaze on *End of the Trail*,
now standing in the beautiful Payne-Kirkpatrick Memorial
Building, that I experienced the night I saw it in Mooney
Grove Park, bathed in the blue-white iridescence of California moonlight. I vowed then to do everything in my
power to help save this great symbol of the tragic fate of
the American Indians. With the help of a great many friends
and generous patrons, we have succeeded.
— Dean Krakel, *End of the Trail: The Odyssey of a Statue*

There was, quite simply, no way to conceive an American
identity without Indians. At the same time, there was no
way to make a complete identity while they remained.
— Philip J. Deloria, *Playing Indian*

IF THEY HADN'T BEEN SQUARE DANCING BENEATH IT, I might
have ignored it. But there they were, the squares of the Central District
Square Dance Association, promenading to and fro in their Kentucky

Colonel bowties and their petticoats, while above them towered the monument, the one with the Indian slumped over his horse.

It's the centerpiece of the National Cowboy & Western Heritage Museum in Oklahoma City, but until that day I'd never seen it in person. Oklahoma City is at one end of the trail, and I've always been at the other. "The West begins here," goes the museum tagline, out here, five miles south of Frontier City, on the edge of the Cross Timbers, on the southern flank of the Great Plains. In the glass atrium that houses it, James Earle Fraser's *End of the Trail* is unmistakable yet out of context, like a celebrity you might encounter in an airport passing.

Like any monument, it looks captive indoors. At 18 feet tall minus pedestal, it soars in reverse. The horse and rider feel as if they've landed there from the ether, their collective slump caught in an embrace of downward pull. The Indian cradles the spear, versus wields it, all but disarmed. That is not a word I choose without trepidation, for decades of critics and commentators, skeptics and sculptors, have seen in Fraser's statue the fate of the Native carved into history, and the saga of the West uniquely spelled out. It's an awful weight to carry for a piece of plaster, however large.

"It's considered pastiche," said Don Reeves, curator and McCasland Chair of Cowboy Culture at the National Cowboy & Western Heritage Museum. "It's been broken so many times and put back together. No telling how much of the amount of original material is left in it. High school kids ran off with the spear a time or two. It wasn't ever created to be a formal, finished work of art."

Created when Fraser was a student in a Chicago art studio, it was a model, sculpted of plaster and entered in the 1898 American Art Association competition in Paris, where it won best of show. In 1915, after years of fine-tuning a model, Fraser exhibited the piece in the Panama-Pacific International Exposition, the San Francisco fair whose memory survives in the monumental Palace of Fine Arts. It placed first again, among 1,500 other sculptures, to the chagrin of the artist Alexander Stirling Calder, who was installed in conflicting roles as both chief sculptor of the exhibition and its contest judge.

"In front of the court of flowers," Calder wrote in a review, "an equestrian statue of the 'American Indian' of unusual significance by Mr.

James Earle Fraser of New York City is placed." Another critic wrote that the work was "meaningful and strong," but that it would lose impact when viewed elsewhere and out of context. The statue was placed in front of the Palace of Jewels in anticipation of its best-of-show crowning

Criticism aside, the statue had struck a chord with the public. Without Fraser's permission or consent, photographs, bookends, ashtrays, and picture books were printed featuring the image; hastily produced postcards of the *End of the Trail* began zipping their way across the continent.

This was not the fate Fraser had intended. He wanted it to stand at Presidio Point, overlooking the Golden Gate, where, last summer, Oracle Team USA sailed its $200 million catamaran to take another America's Cup. He wanted it bronzed, but San Francisco was too cash-poor in 1915, and too cowboy, to pay for it. In the end, he would have settled for a cut of the merch.

"I have been told more than $250,000 worth of prints and photographs were sold of the statue," Fraser wrote in his letters. "Who got the money, I don't know. I do know I didn't get any of it. As a matter of fact, everyone knew of the statue, but no one seemed to know its sculptor."

Indeed, Fraser—and certainly his statue—lacked a certain Westward-ho. Another bid was made for Presidio Point by a sculptor backed by the Automobile Club of California, a piece titled *Covered Wagon 49ers*. In the end, casting anything in bronze had become prohibitive in the heady scrap-heap days of World War I. The award-winning *End of the Trail*, and all the sculptures it had bested, fell into obscurity, tossed en masse into what one local newspaperman called a "graveyard of statues in the Marina Mud."

If he couldn't claim any royalties, Fraser at least wanted his work back. A full decade after San Francisco, he wrote to the director of the de Young Museum of Art: "As it was made of plaster, I presume it did not last long... I would appreciate it if you can tell me whether it bears an inscription of any kind including the title, 'End of the Trail,' my name, and the copyright marking consisting of 'c' within a circle, which I am accustomed to using."

But even as the Auto Club of California folks hemmed and hawed around Fraser's *Trail*, support came from the public, emboldening Fraser's efforts to claim his own. "The public has taken your work deeply into their hearts," one letter read, "and they are interested in you."

"Best I can say is," Reeves said, "he recognized, and many do, on the historical side, what the work came to symbolize, as an icon, an image of the American West. Not as a work of art but as a symbol of the plight.

"Plight—not defeat."

But the *End of the Trail* wasn't in the Marina Mud, or anywhere else in San Francisco. Four years after the expo, the city of Visalia, California, 200-plus miles away in the heart of the San Joaquin Valley, came and got it for $400. And there it stood for 50 years in a city park, periodic coats of paint keeping it respectable, until a fan of Fraser's and then-director at Gilrease Museum acquired the Fraser studio collection for his new post, the National Cowboy Hall of Fame in Oklahoma City.

How it got there is an odyssey of chutzpah and horse-trading.

HEAVY BONES, BIG FEET

Visalia straddles California 99, a string of a highway strung with such knots—Bakersfield, Merced, Modesto, Stockton, Chico. They are one-horse towns (the horse being the vast agriculture of the Central Valley) defined by Sacramento native Joan Didion as towns of "Valley sadness."

"They hint," she wrote, "at evenings spent hanging around gas stations, and suicide pacts sealed in drive-ins."

Visalia is where Tulsa-born photographer Larry Clark Filmed *Ken Park*, its suicidal opening scene shot in Provident Skate Park. *End of the Trail* was standing (and decaying) in Mooney Grove Park when a Western-art aficionado named Dean Krakel found and resurrected it.

In 1963, Krakel left his director's chair at Gilcrease to help the National Cowboy Hall build its coffers. "He was a music man," said Reeves, who joined the museum in 1979. "You remember the movie *Music Man*? The guy who comes into the community getting things going, even if he had to bend a few rules." Before he left Gilcrease, though, Krakel paid a visit to Laura Gardin Fraser, widow of James Earle, to discuss acquiring, and preserving for posterity, the contents of their Connecticut studio.

Five years into Krakel's tenure at the Cowboy Hall, he learned from a friend of the Frasers the whereabouts of the statue. The discovery lit a fire in him. In the preface to his book *End of the Trail: The Odyssey of a Statue*, Krakel said the acquisition of the piece took "years filled with controversy, professional and financial risk, drama, frustration, and ultimately great satisfaction."

"The decision to move an aging 55-year-old plaster statue a distance of 1,500 miles by truck with the intention of performing major restoration work appeared at times not to have been one of my brightest ideas."

But Krakel was the new kid in town, and he felt compelled to put his stamp on the place. The National Cowboy Hall of Fame (as it was then called) was in expansion mode, having acquired, with Krakel's help, the bulk of the Fraser studio collection from Syracuse University. The 140-piece ensemble includes James' model for the *Pioneer Woman*,[1] Laura's *Oklahoma Run*, and even their rule and level. But the collection, in Krakel's mind, was without its gem.

"In spite of the loss of detail and a number of fissures caused by surface deterioration," Krakel wrote, "the statue was the most moving creation I had ever seen. The defeat of the Indian is totally embodied in the figure."

Krakel's curatorial eye for design was keen, and he noted in his first viewing of the statue—on a pedestal inside a reflecting pool, surrounded

---

1   Fraser was among the artists (along with Alexander Stirling Calder, John Gregory, and Hermon Atkins MacNeil) commissioned by Ponca City oilman E.W. Marland to sculpt "a memorial to the pioneer mothers," the winner of which would be installed in the Cherokee Outlet, a rectangle of land bordering Kansas and running between roughly Enid and Woodward. The winning model, by Bryant Baker, is a Ponca City landmark and Oklahoma icon. Fraser's *Affectionate*—with her hair straight, long, and pushed upward by a scarf that appears to lengthen her neck in a way reminiscent of the coiled rings worn by some Zimbabwean women; her strong nose that seems to sniff the prairie air for both harm and opportunity; her long-fingered hands that support the babe who sucks at the breast laid bare from a thin blouse that wrinkles on her shoulders; and the rifle barrel cradled under her left arm—could be mistaken for an Indian. Syracuse University's Martin H. Bush, writing in a 1969 Kennedy Galleries catalogue, said it eloquently captured "the frantic alarm of Indian raids." In a small, separate study of the statue, Fraser's woman braces the shoulders of a young boy now old enough to stand. Her look is straight ahead, and her breast tucked away.

by evergreens—the *End of the Trail*'s geometric balance and simplicity, and the harmonic line in the verticality of the downward-pointed spear. He found in the horse's swollen eye,[2] wind-blown tail, and slightly raised hoof a feeling "of almost unbearable pain."

After meeting with his contact at Tulare County Parks' board, with whom he was negotiating for the statue, Krakel went back to see the piece again. Alone, at 3 a.m., in the glow of moonlight, he fell hard. "As I studied it, I could not help recalling the words of Plenty Coups, the Absarokee (Crow) chief: 'I may be gone, my father, when you return here. I am anxious to go where I may live again as men were intended to live. My bones are heavy and my feet large. But I know justice and tried all my life to be just, even to those who have taken away my old life that was so good. My whole thoughts are of my people. I want them to be healthy, to become again the race they have been.'"

It's as if Krakel had gone Quixote and found his beloved Dulcinea. There, in the moonlight of Mooney Grove, the *End of the Trail* transformed, in his mind, from lost relic to patriotic shrine. The hallmark of the Fraser collection, he wrote, "suddenly became an epitaph of national importance, a monument to all Indians, to their nobility as well as to their tragedy." Convinced of the piece's artistic merit and historic significance, and of his fated role as guardian angel, Krakel carried out his destiny. "Before me was a treasure that I vowed should be preserved for America."

Krakel left the park exhilarated and, for the first time, a little panicked. He was about to spend on one piece more than he already owed Laura Fraser for her whole studio ensemble. In what would become

---

2   The horse's eye is in post-modernist painter Fritz Scholder's *End of the Trail*, which hangs in the Swannie Zink American Indian Galleries at Philbrook Museum of Art, is equally swollen. It's as if Scholder has repossessed Fraser's warrior, and the horse he rode in on. Fraser had depicted Native America at its low point, and Scholder was offering a counter. "The sculpture," said Christina Burke, curator of Native-American and non-Western art at Philbrook Museum, "represents the perceived last days of that traditional way of life, which was irreparably changed by non-Natives who tamed the wild West, its land and its people. Scholder re-appropriated this iconic image for his own purpose, turning the idea of the vanishing Indian on its head."

classic Krakel fashion, he always preferred two birds in the bush to one in hand.

"When he set his mind to bring a new exhibition," Reeves said, "it was visionary, bold to the extreme. He'd tell the board, 'Why do we do this? It needs to be done!' With Visalia, it was, 'We'll give you a bronze casting, bring (renowned mold-maker) Cesare Contini in from New York City, go have it cast in Italy, place it in your park, and then it will survive.

"And you give us this plaster casting created in 1915."

Krakel was originally dealing with Visalia about a concrete repro-duction. It didn't matter that their plaster statue was falling into the fountain. The mere idea of concrete hit home with a resounding thud. All of a sudden, Fraser's studio model, until then an object of decay and neglect, became high art. Wrote one local in a letter to the editor: "The difference between an original Rembrandt, a Renoir, a Van Gogh, or a Michelangelo and a copy printed in full color is the same difference there will be between the original statue and its cement copy."

Fairly quickly into the deal, realizing it was about to go south, Krakel upped the ante and promised Visalia a bronze[3]—a Cadillac on a Corolla budget.

OF 'UNUSUAL SIGNIFICANCE'

In his letters, James Earle Fraser, chronicling his adolescent days in the Dakotas, wrote of a hunchback who would sit on his porch carv-ing chalkstone into abstract forms. Fraser would walk by on his way home from school. The stone came from a nearby quarry. "It was east

---

3 Curiously, Krakel offers two varying accounts of his original correspondence with the powers that be in Visalia. On page 96 of his *End of the Trail*, he cites a letter he wrote to the board: "On February 2, 1968, I wrote: I would like to come there and meet with you and members of your Parks and Recreation Board to discuss the possibility of our trading a concrete model for yours..." But, in his book *Adventures in Western Art*, published four years later, the "concrete model" is now a "bronze model." Revisionist history or lapse of memory, Krakel had already built a national shrine around what was essen-tially a lost cause. He was bound to be enamored.

of Mitchell toward the Jim River," Fraser wrote, and it produced a soft stone that worked like cheese and hardened with age.

Though his father, a railroad man, wanted his son to study engineering, Fraser's right-brain tendencies were powerful. Ultimately, he brought both minds together in a career as audacious in its output as artistic in its merits. Yet, unlike the Morans and Turners, Russells and Remingtons of the Western oeuvre, Fraser's name fails to resonate far outside the annals of art history, in spite of his output.

Fraser produced some 500 works in his career, including bronzes, marbles, original plasters, myriad prints, coins, medals, and paintings. He designed the iconic Buffalo nickel, which is also called the Indian-head nickel, given the profile that adorns its obverse (heads), versus the bison on the reverse (tails). It's his Theodore Roosevelt equestrian that guards the Museum of Natural History in New York, the one that comes to life in the form of Robin Williams in *Night at the Museum.*

The historian Frederick Jackson Turner draws the line of frontier encroachment at the hands of industrial expanse at 1890. He delivered his theory in an 1893 address to the American Historical Association of Chicago titled "The Significance of the Frontier in American History," now known as the "Turner Thesis." A year later, at the age of 17, Fraser molded his first *End of the Trail.* He wrote that it came from an idea that had been haunting him since childhood: "Often hunters, wintering with the Indians, stopped over to visit my grandfather on their way south and in that way I heard many stories about the Indians. On one occasion a fine fuzzy bearded old hunter remarked with some bitterness in his voice, 'The Injuns will be driven into the Pacific Ocean.'"

Fraser wasn't the only immigrant son to confront the shifting landscape of the American West through artistic self-expression. Documenting the so-called end of the American Indian, in both word and image, was a turn-of-the-century rite of passage for a good many American artists and writers.

"We construct identity by finding ourselves in relation to an array of people," wrote historian Philip J. Deloria, a Dakota, "and objects who are not ourselves." There's a term of art for it: "Salvage ethnography—the capturing of an authentic culture thought to be rapidly and inevitably disappearing—has from the beginning been haunted by fractures of

logic." Meaning, it might be more romantic, and certainly more convenient, to depict the conquered Native atop a prairie pony, armed with
quill and bow, than on a metropolitan street corner sporting a jean
jacket. (I still remember the queasiness I felt when my brother showed
me an album he'd just bought on vinyl, *Ed Ames Sings Ed Ames*, which
warped forever my vision of Ames' Mingo, the Cherokee sidekick to
Fess Parker's Daniel Boone.)

Fraser writes in his papers of the Black Hills of his transient youth,
a region and an era he shared with nearby Sioux children, if through
the lens of a resident alien: "Each night, we were surrounded by packs
of wolves. Their mournful howling caused my spine to tingle and im-
pressed upon me the lonely vastness of the West." A loneliness Fraser
tried to channel, exacerbated by the disappearing Indian.

"In conjunction with Indian removal," wrote Deloria, "popular
American imagery began to play on earlier symbolic linkages between
Indians and the past, and these images eventually produced the full-
blown ideology of the vanishing Indian, which proclaimed it foreor-
dained that less-advanced societies should disappear in the presence of
those more advanced."

Those then coloring history—Cooper's *Last of the Mohicans*, you
could argue—turned from the Manifest Destiny policies of Washington to the tribes themselves, as if the proof of vanquish was somehow
inherent in the pudding. But even Washington itself wanted to wax
poetic. "'By a law of nature,'" Deloria quotes Supreme Court Justice
Joseph Story, speaking in 1828, "'they seem destined to a slow, but sure
extinction. Everywhere, at the approach of the white man, they fade
away. We hear the rustling of their footsteps, like that of the withered
leaves of autumn, and they are gone forever. They pass mournfully by
us, and they return no more.'"

This premature death rattle is what fueled Krakel's imagination. But,
in spite of the years of deterioration and abuse that wore on the *End of
the Trail*, the citizens of Visalia—some of them, anyway—felt equally
compelled by the monument's significance and protested vehemently,
in jingoistic letters to the editor, of this cowboy from the plains who'd
come to steal their Indian.

"We've awakened," one of them wrote, "to the value of something we've got."

THE RAPE OF MOONEY GROVE

Krakel's first challenge was getting the thing out of the park, and in one piece.

A San Francisco philanthropist who recalled the statue's dominance at the Palace of Fine Arts offered to have a bronze casting made of the original, in the interest of keeping the *End of the Trail* in California. As Krakel brought out colleagues from Oklahoma City to begin surveying the feasibility of such a move, local opposition began to swell.

"If the board gives (it) away in exchange for a cement copy," an editorial quotes one reader, "the rape of Mooney Grove will certainly go down in history as one of the most stupid acts of this or any other board in Tulare County."

The groundswell compelled Krakel to revise his original offer from concrete to bronze. This would be news to the museum board in Oklahoma City. But with an agreement on paper, Krakel called in his staff at the Cowboy Hall to study how best to move the statue without losing it. Given the settling and surface cracks, and the still unknown composition of the plaster itself, lifting it in one piece was overruled in favor of cutting the Indian off at the waist. Shipping crates would be built to transport the two crated pieces on a flatbed from the Central Valley to Oklahoma City. As the first cuts were made, Krakel and team held its collective breath. "The torso swung in a wide, easy, breathtaking arc," he wrote, "gently rocking to a fro like a chair on a Ferris wheel."

Not far into the trip, Krakel got a call from the dispatcher of the trucking firm doing the hauling: The *End of the Trail* was coming to pieces. Half the Indian's face and most of his chest had been crushed. Richard Muno, museum curator, bought three tons of sawdust to stuff inside the crate, cushioning the crumbling plaster. Leonard McMurry, an Oklahoma sculptor charged with the project, assured Krakel that, if the pieces could remain relatively intact, restoration would be a cinch. "Shucks, Dean," he said, " it won't be anything at all to restore it if I can hang onto the pieces." Reporters from Los Angeles and San Francisco, having gotten wind, began to ring Krakel back home.

They were the least of those he had to answer to. In addition to the $475,000 he'd paid Laura Gardin Fraser for her studio, Krakel was budgeting another $250,000 for a building to house the *End of the Trail*, a statue whose value he was calculating at $330,000, based on acquisition and moving costs, insurance, restoration and maintenance. It was enough, for now, to just unveil the thing, which the museum did in late May 1968, after McMurry had stabilized it. Philanthropist and Navy man John E. Kirkpatrick—named "Oklahoma's Admiral for the Arts" in a newspaper headline—spoke, and was followed by tribal elders, who "chanting, symbolically proclaimed the arrival of one who had come from great distances to the land of Oklahoma."

The veil was pulled from the *End of the Trail*, revealing a statue that had sagged 14 inches since its placement at the Palace of Jewels in 1915. Inside the cavity were the blackened wicks of alcohol-burning candles, sealed inside the plaster more than 50 years ago, to ensure that the plaster would cure.

Mooney Grove would wait three years for its casting. In the meantime, Krakel began fundraising for the cash to pay for the bronze and for the building that would house his original. Half the funding came from Kirkpatrick, a decorated Navy man who made a fortune in steel and then oil, and the other half from one Nona Payne, the widow of a Pampa, Texas, rancher. At the 1970 dedication of the Payne-Kirkpatrick Memorial Building,[4] John Tower, the first the Republican U.S. senator to hail from Texas since Reconstruction, gave a nod to David Payne, "paying tribute to the West Texas rancher for his vision, frugality, and devotion to his state and country."

---

4 It's now an exhibit for youth called the Children's Cowboy Corral. The *End of the Trail* now stands in the atrium designed for it in a museum expansion in the late 1990s. Thanks to the oversight of one Duane Cartier, a visiting curator, the statue is now surfaced in a white silica sealed by the application of a solvent. "The Germans created it to put on buildings," said current curator Don Reeves. "Up in the Alps. You know those alpine houses with the broad wooden beams surrounded by white plaster? They came up with a treatment that was impervious to external deprivation." In front of the *End of the Trail* are two interpretive panels, 30 by 40 inches each, presenting what Reeves called "the artist's view and the historical view."

Hollywood leading man Joel McCrea, a Cowboy Museum trustee, introduced Tower. In a photo of the proceedings, McCrea sits off to the far left, studying his lines. At the podium is Jasper Ackerman, another benefactor, while at the far right, a bored-looking, bespectacled Krakel stares out of the frame. The *End of the Trail* looms as large as ever, larger, behind a fresh veil of glass and steel.

On the podium, facing the audience, is a drawing of what appears to be another *End of the Trail*. Upon closer inspection, the horse is bucking, not sulking, and the rider—maybe an Indian, maybe a cowboy, or even a headless rider, so obscure is the figure—is doing his best to stay in the saddle.

THIS IS THE END

Gilcrease Museum presented a show in 1985, *James Earle Fraser: Sculptor of American Heroes*. Julie Pearson, writing in a March 1985 article in *Uptown News*, pounced on the retrospective, attacking Fraser's depiction of the American Indian and even his horse, which "also seems to be on its last leg."

"But while the beaten Indian may have had his turn-of-the-century appeal, the image should now be seen for what it is—a false image that gratifies the public's desire for breast-beating while at the same time reinforcing its notions of cultural superiority." Pulling no punches, Pearson mocked Fraser for depicting "Manifest Destiny, roughrider machismo, or war as a noble cause."

That 1985 exhibition was a co-presentation of Gilcrease and Syracuse University, original keeper of the Fraser flame. Some of the works on display were even for sale. The catalogue included a "Retail Price List for James Earle Fraser Bronzes, with Tax," offering a dozen replicas of *Study of Thomas Jefferson* for $12,720 each (Gilcrease edition) and 10 seated *Lincoln* copies for $11,660 a pop (Syracuse exhibit, and the same price put on 11 replicas of *Pioneer Woman*). Also in the Syracuse show were 34 examples of *End of the Trail*, ranging in size from 12 to 34 inches and costing between $6,360 and $18,020.

Fraser designed more patriotic sculptures than any other artist in America, and created one of the more iconic images of an American

Indian that we possess. In molding mud, with his hands, Fraser made it his métier to wrestle down a version of American history he could live with. Among award-winning sculptures and designs that included the statues at the entrance of the Lincoln Memorial, the Navy Cross, and a medal awarded by a group called the American Committee for Relief of Devastated France, he crafted the two works for which he is best known, or should be, anyway: the Indian-head nickel and his *End of the Trail*. Indian as currency, and enigma.

One I have in the top shelf of my bedroom dresser, in with a fistful of other yen I've kept for some curious reason or other, none of them being value. In time—and it took some time—Fraser saw his other monumental work cast in metal. In addition to the Krakel gift that adorns Mooney Grove Park, *End of the Trail* stands in bronze in the city of Waupun, Wisconsin, bestowed there by Clarence Shaler, an inventor who made his fortune in vulcanized rubber tire patches. Shaler had seen the statue on its pedestal at the San Francisco expo.

"It serves as more than a thing of beauty," said F.T. Clark, town mayor, at the unveiling. "It seems fitting that the *End of the Trail* should be placed in Waupun, which is known as 'Early Dawn,' thus completing the beginning and end of the Indians' day."

In 1975, Dean Krakel, now firmly in the saddle, began a conquest of a different sort, venting his frustrations at the metric system, a conversion he considered obtrusive at least and, at worst, an un-American activity. On the heels of Congress passing the Metric Conversion Act, Krakel, unconvinced of metric's popularity, conducted his own poll and mounted a defense of traditional weights and measures. "At my own expense," he told a reporter with the *Daily Oklahoman*, "I sent a trained historian to the Bureau of Standards to review the original studies. But they had already destroyed their records. To me this is worse than Watergate."

"We wear 10-gallon hats," he said, "not 10-liter hats. Nine hundred million people are using Chinese. Why don't we switch to the Chinese language?"

Krakel said he'd received letters from Canadians who told him the conversion has cost their country much confusion and money. The Canadian Broadcasting Corporation, in 1977, asked him why the zeal, noting on the airwaves that he'd been "conducting his campaign from the headquarters of the Cowboy Hall Fame."

"It's in keeping with the Marxist doctrine of one world, one monetary system, one language, one educational system," Krakel said. "It's anti-Christ, this one weights and measurements, in this philosophical way the Communist wants one of everything. We're Americans. We're different. And we did it by the inch, by the yard, by the mile." By the end of the interview, the DJ could only chuckle.

Krakel's campaign ways got the best of him, and by the early 1980s he was out at the hall. Then, in April 1985, Krakel used a proxy-vote maneuver to reclaim operational control of the museum, in defiance of several prominent board members, who retired on the spot, among them Edward L. Gaylord, publisher of the *Oklahoman*; Dean A. McGee, honorary chairman and director of Kerr-McGee Corporation; Ardmore oilman Sam Noble; and Dale E. Mitchell, chairman of the board of Citizens National Bank.

"This action today, which could destroy the Hall, was instigated by Krakel and a dissident group of out-of-state directors led by Frank Leu, an insurance man from Tennessee, and Ed Rutherford, a cattle feeder from California," said Gaylord in a statement to his own newspaper. "Both Rutherford and Leu are good businessmen and friendly fellows, but entirely ignorant of the local situation regarding Dean Krakel.

"Krakel is an outstanding expert in appraising and selling Western art, probably the best in the country. His ability as an administrator and a business manager is near zero."

"It was sort of like a coup that might take place in a banana republic," Mitchell, the museum's treasurer, told the *New York Times*.

In defense, Krakel filed a libel and slander suit against Gaylord and other board members, accusing them of conspiring to ruin him by spreading false statements about him, and seeking $35 million in damages. An attorney for the defendants called the suit "woefully inadequate."

In 1988, Krakel filed for bankruptcy. He died July 2, 1998.

"The Cowboy Hall of Fame folks who hired my dad had no clue about Western art and didn't know anything about Fraser or the *End of the Trail*," said Krakel's son, Dean, a Denver-based photojournalist.

"He brought all of that to the empty shell that was the CBHF. They hired him because of his vision and his can-do attitude. He had this incredible passion for the West, a knowledge of its history, a love for its art and artists, and this amazing dream and vision.

"What is more, the ability to inspire others so that they jumped on his train and went along for the ride. And, hey, they built the damn train and the tracks as well."

In 1880, when Fraser was four years old, his father, Thomas Alexander Fraser, moved the family to Deadwood, South Dakota, blazing a trailhead for his employer, the Chicago-Milwaukee Railroad. The eight years that young Fraser spent on the prairie informed his work thereafter.

Dean Krakel ended his career as director of the High Plains Western Heritage Center in Spearfish, 15 miles north of Deadwood, on a feeder creek of the Redwater River, itself a tributary of the Missouri River. The High Plains motto is "… How time flies."

HAPPY TRAILS

Once you start looking for it, it's everywhere.

It's the logo for Saylor's End of the Trail Stable in Walkerton, Indiana. "Leaving camp for the wide open spaces," with Fraser's subject silhouetted against a red-orange mesa. There is an End of the Trail Cabinet Company in Merced, California, an hour and half north of Visalia.

It's for sale at The Cheap Place Patches and Gifts ("Let's talk about Patches"). "Some people really like Native American art, especially the popular *End of the Trail* statue." At an online shop called The Flag Makers, you can buy it emblazoned across an American flag of 3-by-5-foot polyester and inked with UV inhibitors "to make sure your colors last."

It's in a free pattern at Stallings Stained Glass of Swartz Creek, Michigan, and on the broad back of a customer of Masterpiece Tattoo & Body Piercing of Salem, New Hampshire, inked against a billowing tuft of cloud.

You can buy it on a belt buckle from Just Buckles: "Dejected American native sits astride a horse while a native face looks into the future.

Eagles fly in this sepia gradient rectangular framed belt buckle that remembers America's history."

A group of Georgia rockers called the End of the Trail Band played a reunion show last March at a club called the End of the Trail Saloon. "The End of the Trail is not only a band, it is a family, and a life's long story." It's on the cover of the Beach Boys 1971 album *Surf's Up*, which leads with a song called "Don't Go Near the Water."

It's in my own house, under my own nose, sewn onto a blanket tucked away in a closet, a keepsake, and on the cover of my wife's Owasso Rams diploma.[5]

It's *not* included in the "20 Objects That Shape Oklahoma" spread published in the August 2014 issue of *Oklahoma Magazine*, nor is anything else from the National Cowboy museum. But it's beyond object, printed on shot glasses, ball caps, phone protectors, wall clocks, earrings, and bookends. Wikipedia calls one version of it "the original bronze replica," an electronic footnote to its mongrel pedigree.

At Lyon's Indian Store, you can buy it on a puzzle or a postcard or, for a few dollars more, as a small copper statuette with a young Indian woman bowing elegantly in place of Fraser's buckled warrior. The serenity on her face, with the fluorescent light reflecting off the polished metal, is almost sweet.

My mother-in-law owns two small replicas of *End of the Trail*, one of which sits on her coffee table. In the 18 years I've been visiting there, I'd never noticed it.

I'd been working at Philbrook a year and a half before I saw Fritz Scholder's *The End of the Trail*, 1970. It hangs on a column in the small, contemporary room of the Zink Galleries. To get to it, I have to descend two flights of Italian Renaissance, English Romanticism, and colonial portraiture.

---

5 *Owasso* is a tribal term meaning "end of the trail." Some sources say Osage, but "I don't think it's Osage," said Tahlequah-born, Pawhuska-bred Ryan Red Corn. "Sometimes those places get written down wrong. That don't mean they weren't over there. We have other names that match up. *Tasilatawa* is what we call Tulsa. 'O' designates the result of something. I just don't know about Owasso. It just doesn't pull together." Red Corn, in addition to being a student of Osage place names, runs an ad agency called Buffalo Nickel Creative.

Scholder's painting of a sculpture adds a formidable wrinkle to the canon of the Trail. Of course, by 1970, Fraser's mark with the statue had been set in proverbial stone. Scholder was painting *End of the Trail* not in tribute but in effigy, and was as likely riffing off a shot glass, or a motel sign, or an album cover. Either way, from somewhere subconscious, the one frontier that never closes.

"Painting today is probably even more important than ever before," Scholder said in a 1996 interview, "but the artist really must have something to say, about whatever subject, because every subject is a cliché."

INDEX

BY AUTHOR

BY ISSUE NUMBER